18/13

INFANTRY UNIFORMS

INCLUDING ARTILLERY AND OTHER SUPPORTING TROOPS OF BRITAIN AND THE COMMONWEALTH

INFANTRY UNIFORMS

INCLUDING ARTILLERY AND OTHER
SUPPORTING TROOPS OF BRITAIN AND
THE COMMONWEALTH
1742–1855
in colour

by
ROBERT and CHRISTOPHER
WILKINSON-LATHAM

Illustrated by
JACK CASSIN-SCOTT

The Notes on Weapons specially written for this
Volume by Major John Wilkinson-Latham

BLANDFORD PRESS

LONDON

First published 1969

Illustration copyright © 1969 Blandford Press

Text copyright © R. & C. WILKINSON-LATHAM

Notes on Weapons copyright © MAJOR J. WILKINSON-LATHAM

SBN 7137 05078

Colour printed in Great Britain by Colour Reproductions Ltd.,
Billericay. Text set in Monotype Times New Roman, printed and bound in
Great Britain by Richard Clay (The Chaucer Press), Ltd., Bungay, Suffolk

PREFACE

With this volume on Infantry, from 1742 to 1855, we have followed the same pattern of information and illustrations as in our previous volume on Cavalry Uniforms. The selection of the uniforms again gives a cross-section of the typical and the unusual. Contemporary pictures and prints have been selected as the subject, supported by any written contemporary evidence. In order to allow more space on each illustration for close-ups of shakos, belt plates and other details, we have devoted six plates entirely to weapons. We have tried to cater for many types of enthusiasts. Primarily, we think, it will appeal to the model-soldier devotee. Those too whose business is research for film and stage will, we hope, find it a helpful reference. Last, but by no means least, it should be a fascinating study for admirers of military pageantry from the ages of 7 to 70.

We wish to thank the following either for providing information or allowing us to examine items in their collections:

W. Y. Carman of the National Army Museum
Capt. Hollies Smith of Parker Galleries
D. Leech of Henry Potter & Co.
Colonel Nicolson of *Tradition*
H.M. Tower of London
National Army Museum

Our thanks to Mrs. M. H. Craven for again patiently typing and retyping the manuscript. To our mother who, as in the previous volume, was a source of encouragement to us both.

ROBERT WILKINSON-LATHAM
CHRISTOPHER WILKINSON-LATHAM

Cannes, 06,
France

INTRODUCTION

The period covered by this book, 1742–1855, spans an era in which the armies of Great Britain and its Empire were engaged in practically all continents in the world.

The Battle of Dettingen on 16 June 1743 was the last battle in which the King of England was present in person and also the last in which the Order of Knighthood was conferred on the field of battle. At the close of the battle the heroism of Trooper Brown of the 3rd Dragoons was recognised by King George II, and he was dubbed Knight Banneret.

During these 100 years of fighting the backbone of the Army was the infantry, known affectionately as the footslogger or P.B.I. ('poor bloody infantry'), and on the regimental colours names like Minden (1 August 1759), the Peninsular War (1808–14), Waterloo (18 June 1815), India (1818–26), Afghanistan (1839–42), China (1840–42) and the Crimea (1854–55) are proudly borne as a tribute to the valour of the men of the regiments concerned in those particular battles.

When Louisberg was captured from the French on 25 July 1758 fourteen battalions of infantry, comprising 12,000 all ranks, took part, and suffered casualties of approximately 5 per cent of the force, and the honour LOUISBERG is now borne by the 1st Royal Scots, 15th East Yorks., 17th Leicester, 22nd Cheshire, 28th Gloucester, 35th Royal Sussex, 40th South Lancs., 45th Sherwood Foresters, 27th North Lancs., 48th Northamptons, 58th Northamptons, 60th King's Royal Rifles and the 62nd Wiltshire, serving as marines. The 78th of Foot were also engaged, having more casualties than any other battalion, but the regiment was disbanded soon afterwards. It was again raised by Lord Seaforth in 1793 as the 78th Highlanders, but this honour was not conferred on the new battalion.

It was not until the Battle of Waterloo that the practice of rewarding soldiers with a medal to commemorate their presence at a particular battle was introduced fully throughout the Army. In commemoration of the victories in the Peninsula during the years 1808 and 1809 two gold medals were struck and awarded only to officers. The larger is $2\frac{1}{8}$ in. in diameter, and the ribbon is decorated with gold bars 2 in. long and $\frac{5}{8}$ in. wide, bearing the names of the battles for which they were given. The smaller gold medal, $1\frac{3}{8}$ in. in diameter, was given to field officers and those who actually commanded a battalion during the engagement. The medal was also granted for engagements in the East Indies and North America.

Many officers were entitled to more than one medal, and with the number of bars they became an inconvenient appendage. It was therefore ordered that one medal only should be worn by each officer and the number of bars limited to two. Upon a claim to a third bar the medal ceased to be worn, and in its place the Peninsular Gold Cross was awarded. For subsequent battles bars were awarded to the Gold Cross.

Of the Peninsular medal, 469 were issued without bars, 143 with one bar and 72 with two bars, and of the Gold Cross, 61 without bars, 46 with one bar, 18 with two bars, 17 with three bars, 8 with four bars, 7 with five bars, 3 with six bars, 2 with seven bars and only one with nine bars, which belonged to the Duke of Wellington.

Infantry regiments also took great pride in their regimental nicknames, many of which were won on the field of battle during this period. The Fighting Fifth (Northumberland Fusiliers) obtained this soubriquet during the Peninsular War, where their casualties numbered 18 officers and 420 other ranks. The Holy Boys (9th Norfolk) also got this name in the Peninsular War, where their cap badge, featuring Britannia, was mistaken by the Spaniards for the Virgin Mary. The 17th Leicester acquired their nickname, the Bengal Tigers, on account of their services in India, where the battalion was stationed for twenty years from 1804 to 1823. At Alexandria in 1801 the 28th Gloucester became known as the Back Numbers, later changed to Back Badgers when regimental badges took the place of numbers: they placed their regimental number on the back of their caps as well as the front, so that the enemy attacking on both sides would think that all the men were facing their way.

The Worcestershire Regiment (29th of Foot) were massacred in North America in 1746 when caught at Mess without their weapons, and from then on officers have always worn swords in the Mess, hence their name, the Ever-sworded. The 57th Middlesex have, ever since the Battle of Albuhera (16 May 1811), been known as the Die-Hards: their commander, Colonel Inglis, lay dying on the field, shouting, 'Die hard, my men, die hard!'

Other regimental names have come from the colours of the uniform. The 35th Royal Sussex was known as the Orange Lilies, from the facing colour on their jackets; the 47th Loyal North Lancs., the Cauliflowers, from their white facings; the 58th are the Black Cuffs, which is self-explanatory, and the 93rd Argyll & Sutherland Highlanders, the Thin Red Line, for their heroic efforts in the Crimea.

Of other nicknames, perhaps the most indicative of the soldier's sense of humour is the 65th York and Lancaster, whose badge incorporates the Royal tiger and the Union rose, prompting the nickname the Cat and the Cabbage.

At the beginning of this Introduction we said that infantry are the backbone of the Army. This must be so, when one realises that infantry are engaged in almost every battle and, although artillery can force the enemy to retreat from the field and cavalry can gain ground from the enemy, the arm of the service that subsequently holds the ground that is won is the infantry and their mechanical successors.

In the North American War General Wolfe decided to form regiments of specially trained troops for scouting and skirmishing. These became known as Light Infantry, and adopted the badge of a stringed bugle horn, because in the scouting role they moved in extended order far in advance of the remainder of the army and could no longer be controlled by the drum, as were other battalions of infantry. Their orders were given by the bugle. So effective did these Light Infantry regiments become that each Infantry battalion had a Light Infantry company added to it, in addition to the Grenadier company, whose men were specially trained in the art of handling and throwing grenades. Flank companies, as they became known, remained in existence until they were disbanded in 1862 after the period covered by this book, and their distinctions in dress are shown in certain of the plates.

An important role of the Armed Forces in time of peace is Ceremonial, and the sight of soldiers in full dress, whether in London or in one of the Commonwealth capitals, must stir the heart of every observer. So many of the uniforms worn on these ceremonial occasions derive in origin if not in detail from the colourful period covered by this volume. Perhaps this is part of the 'magic' of the great military parade or Tournament, that it evokes memories of an age when the foot soldiers of the British and Commonwealth Armies wrote pages of not-to-be-forgotten history.

NOTE

The colour Plates and the descriptive text which follows have been placed in date order and not in order of seniority. Where there coincides more than one regiment at any particular date, the following order of precedence has been adopted:

Royal Artillery.
Royal Engineers (Sappers & Miners).
Foot Guards.
Infantry of the Line.
Other Corps.
Volunteers.
Dominion and Commonwealth Troops.

In describing the colour of coats and coatees scarlet has been used for officers and red for other ranks. The colour for corporals and privates was a brick red whereas that of sergeants and above was more scarlet.

2 **1st Foot Guards.** Grenadier 1751

1 **24th Foot**. Private 1742

3　**A Royal Regiment.** Drummer 1751

4 **21st Foot**. Grenadier 1751

5   **24th Foot**. Grenadier 1751

6 **40th Foot.** Grenadier 1751

7   **41st Foot.** Private 1751

8   **42nd Foot.** Grenadier 1751

9　**General Wolfe.** 1759

10 **Royal Artillery.** Officer 1760

11 **27th Foot.** Grenadier 1760

12 **24th Foot**. Grenadier 1768

13 **5th Foot.** Light Infantryman 1771

14 **13th Foot**. Drummer 1771

15 **Queens Rangers, 1st American Regiment of Canada.** Rifleman
1780

16   **87th Foot.** Private 1793

17   **14th Foot.** Private 1794

18 Royal Artillery. Gunner 1797

19 **60th Foot**. Private 1800

20   **Malta Light Infantry.** Private 1800

21 **Bombay Grenadiers**. Sepoy 1800

22 **56th Foot.** Officer 1801

23　**Honourable Artillery Company, Infantry Division.** Private 1803

24　**Duke of Cumberland's Sharpshooters.** Rifleman 1803

25 **45th Foot.** Officer 1804

26 **Honourable Artillery Company, Artillery Division.** Gunner 1804

27 **Malta Military Artificers.** Private 1805

28 **12th Foot.** Private 1806

29　**30th Foot.** Private 1806

30 **35th Foot.** Officer 1806

31　**14th Foot.** Officer Light Company 1807

32　**77th Foot.** Drum Major 1810

33 **Bengal European Regiment.** Private 1811

34 **1st Foot Guards.** Officer 1812

35　**42nd Foot.** Sergeant 1812

36   7th Madras Light Infantry. Havildar 1812

37 **Royal Artillery.** Officer 1815

38 **Lieutenant-General.** 1815

39 **3rd Foot Guards.** Sergeant Light Company 1815

40 **3rd Foot Guards.** Grenadier 1815

41   **7th Foot.** Private 1815

42 **30th Foot.** Officer 1815

43　**33rd Foot.** Pioneer 1815

44 **67th Foot.** Officer 1815

45　**69th Foot**. Private 1815

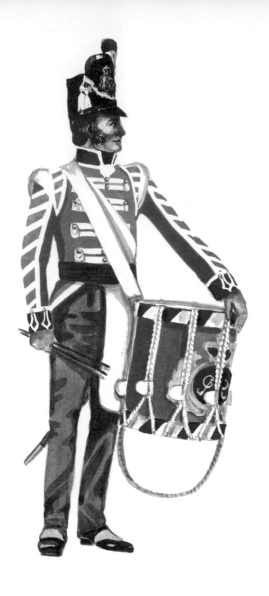

46 **73rd Foot**. Drummer 1815

47   **95th Foot.** Private 1815

48   **Malta Fencible Artillery.** Gunner 1815

49   **Malta Provisional Battalion.**   Officer 1815

50　**West India Regiment.** Private 1815

51 **71st Foot.** Sergeant 1816

52 21st Bengal Native Infantry. Havildar 1819

53 **2nd Foot Guards.** Officer 1821

54 **2nd Foot Guards.** Officer Grenadier Company 1821

55 **91st Foot.** Officer Light Company 1822

56   **77th Foot.** Officer 1823

57 **Royal Artillery.** Officer 1828

58 Royal Sappers & Miners. Officer 1830

59   **6th Foot**. Private 1832

60   **Rifle Brigade.** Rifleman 1832

61   **2nd Foot Guards.** Colour Sergeant 1833

62 **13th Foot.** Sergeant 1833

63 **1st Foot Guards.** Officer 1834

64 **3rd Foot Guards.** Colour Sergeant 1834

65 **Rifle Brigade.** Officer 1834

66   **23rd Foot.**   Regimental Quartermaster Sergeant 1835

67 **2nd Foot Guards.** Negro Bandsman 1836

68   **Royal Artillery.** Officer 1840

69   **24th Foot.** Private 1840

70　**92nd Foot**. Private 1840

71 **Madras Rifles.** Officer 1840

72 **30th Madras Native Infantry.** Officer 1840

73 **Ceylon Regiment.** Naik 1840

74 **Honourable East India Company College, Addiscombe.** Cadet
1844

75　**60th Rifles.** Officer 1845

76   **Hyderabad Artillery.** Officer 1845

77   **65th Bengal Native Infantry.** Sepoy, Light Company 1845

78 **Royal Artillery.** Officer 1846

79   **68th Foot.** Sergeant 1846

80　**92nd Foot.** Officer 1846

81   **Madras Native Infantry.** Band Sergeant 1846

82 **Malta Fencible Regiment.** Private 1847

83   **Honourable Artillery Company.** Infantry Officer 1848

84 **Royal Dockyard Battalion.** Private 1848

85   **Hyderabad Infantry.** Officer 1848

86 **57th Foot.** Private Grenadier Company 1849

87   **7th Foot.** Sergeant Major 1850

88 **74th Foot.** Officer 1850

89   **88th Foot.** Corporal 1854

90   **41st Bengal Native Infantry.** Sepoy 1855

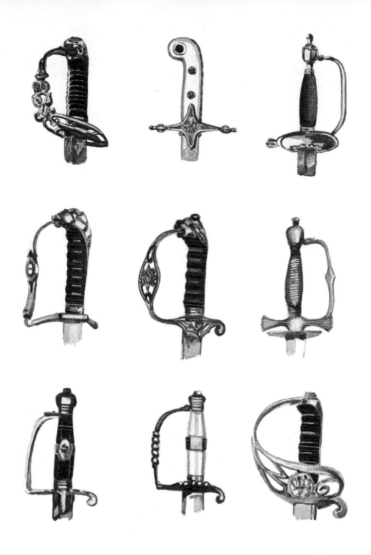

91   A. Sword 1803 Pattern. B. Sword 1831 Pattern for General Officers.
C. Sword 1796 Pattern. D. Sword Grenadier or 1st Foot Guards N.C.O.
1816. E. Sword 3rd or Scots Guards N.C.O. 1803. F. Sword 35th Foot
1780. G. Sword Volunteer 1800. H. Sword 1786 Pattern. I. Sword 1822
Pattern.

92 A. Sword Hilt Royal Engineers 1856. B. Hanger 1742. C. Sword Pioneers 1834. D, E, F. Band Swords. G. Band Sword 1850. H. Hanger Royal Artillery and Artillery. I. Sword Land Transport Corps.

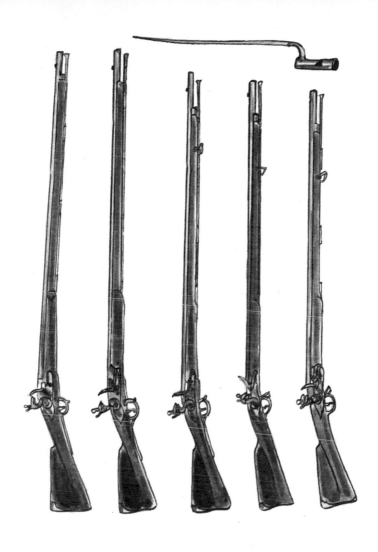

93   A. Long Land Musket 1731. B. Long Land Musket 1746. C. Short Land Musket 1762. D. Light Infantry Musket 1759. E. India Pattern Musket.

94 A. Brunswick Rifle 1847 and Sword Bayonet. B. Baker Rifle 1800 and
Sword Bayonet. (The saw back shown was experimental. Normal was
issue without it.) C. Brunswick Rifle for Sergeants of Foot Guards with
Socket Bayonet. D. Brunswick Rifle 1837 and Sword Bayonet. E. Baker
Rifle 1816 and Socket Bayonet.

95   A. Baker Rifle 1823 and Bayonet. B. Carbine Sappers & Miners 1843 and
Bayonet. C. India Pattern Musket and Bayonet. D. Sergeants Musket
and Bayonet. E. Cadets Musket and Bayonet.

96   A. Enfield Rifle 1853 and Bayonet. B. Musket 1839 and Bayonet.
C. Minie Rifle 1851 and Bayonet. D. Musket 1842 and Bayonet. E.
Lancaster Carbine and Bayonet.

1. 24th Foot. Private, 1742

Head Dress

The head dress worn by Battalion companies of regiments of the Line was a black felt tricorne hat. This was the hat described in the Clothing Warrant of 1742. It was a broad-brimmed black felt hat turned up on both sides and at the back. The front edge was stiffened with bone to give the dipped effect. The brim, in the case of the 24th, was edged in white tape with a black bow and strand of tape and with a button on the left side.

Uniform

The coat was red with green lapels and cuffs but with white turnbacks, which were specially mentioned in the Clothing Warrant of 1742. This was a departure from the general order, as the facings and skirt linings at this period were invariably the same. The lapels, which were buttoned back to the waist, were edged in regimental tape, being white with a central line of willow green. The collar was also edged in tape. The button loops on each lapel were pointed and formed from 2 rows of regimental-pattern tape. There were 3 lines of tape below the lapel at the waist on both sides of the coat. The skirts were buttoned back to reveal the peculiarity of the white facings. In the centre of the skirt on both sides was a central line of regimental tape with 4 tapes running across and a button on each at the intersection. The waistcoat was red, edged in regimental tape. A white stock and shirt were worn. The cuffs were large with a dip in the centre and edged with one row of regimental-pattern tape. Above the cuff at the dip was a further line of tape with 4 tapes running across, with buttons at the intersection. The shoulder-tab of red on the left shoulder held the buff crossbelt in place. The breeches were of red and worn with white gaiters, reaching to above the knee and buttoning on the outside; they were held with black tapes which buckled below the knee.

Accoutrements

A buff shoulder-belt, $2\frac{3}{4}$ in. wide and buckled in the centre, was worn over the left shoulder. Note the absence of a match case – a peculiarity of the Grenadiers. A black pouch containing ammunition, suspended from the right hip. Around the waist was a 2-in. buff belt from which, on the left hip, hung a frog to hold the bayonet and hanger. (This hanger later disappeared for all except Grenadiers.)

Weapons. Musket (Plate 93 A), Bayonet (Plate 93 A), Hanger (Plate 92 B).

2. 1st Foot Guards. Grenadier, 1751

Head Dress

The 'mitre' cap was worn by all Grenadiers at this period. The cap for the 1st Foot Guards had a blue cloth front, 12 in. high, edged in white tape. In the centre was a Garter star, having a red centre and white rays to the star. At each side of the star there were leaves embroidered in white worsted, the whole surmounted by a crown in heraldic colours. The front flap was of red cloth, edged in white tape, with the motto *Nec aspera terrent* below. Underneath this was the white horse of Hanover. The headband at the back was of blue cloth and the top of red, both embroidered with leaves. The cap was completed by a red-and-white tuft on the top.

Uniform

A red coat was worn which, as shown, had the lapels buttoned back to reveal the waistcoat. Lapels and cuffs were of regimental face colour and, in the case of the 1st Foot Guards, this was blue. A white stock and shirt were worn under the waistcoat and showed at the neck. A plain red shoulder-tab was fitted to the left shoulder, which located the shoulder-belt and kept it in place. The lapels were buttoned back to the waist and edged outwardly with white tape, as was the small red collar. The skirts were buttoned back to reveal the blue lining. A pocket flap was situated on both hips, edged in white tape. The lapels were squared off 3 loops from the waist, so that when buttoned over in marching order the top section was double-breasted and the 3 buttons at the bottom single-breasted. The large blue deep cuffs had a dip and were edged with 2 wide rows of regimental tape, with a slashed panel of white tape and buttons above. The waistcoat was red with buttons and tapes and edged all round with white

tape. In the case of the Foot Guards and other Royal regiments, breeches were blue. The white gaiters which buttoned up on the outside and extended above the knee had black tapes and buckles below the knee.

Accoutrements

A 2¾-in. buff leather belt was worn over the left shoulder and fixed with a large brass buckle at the front. A brass match case with chain was fitted above the buckle and contained the match for lighting the grenades. At the end of the belt on the right hip was a large black leather pouch for ammunition, which had a crown surmounting the letters GR fixed to the flap. Around the waist under the coat, when worn open, and over the waistcoat was a 2-in. buff belt buckled at the centre, with a frog on the left hip to carry the bayonet and hanger.

Weapons. Musket (Plate 93 B), Bayonet (Plate 93 B), Hanger (Plate 92 B).

3. A Royal Regiment. Drummer, 1751

Head Dress

The head dress worn by the fifes and drums was the cloth 'mitre' cap. The front was of blue cloth embroidered with a crown in heraldic colours; it was 12 in. high and edged in white tape. Below the crown were crossed flags and drums. The front flap was red, edged in a border lined in white with the motto *Nec aspera terrent*.

Below this was the running horse of Hanover. The cap had a red back, falling on the right side with a white tuft at the top. The headband at the back was blue for Royal regiments and edged on the top in white. Although the band is shown by Morier to be plain, it is thought that there may have been a drum and crossed sticks at the back, or even a regimental number.

Uniform

The Warrant of 1751 stated that drummers of Royal regiments were allowed to wear the Royal livery, and this is shown in Morier's paintings of 1751. The coat was red-lined, faced and lapelled in blue, and laced as shown in Royal lace. The skirts were turned back, revealing the blue lining. A white stock and shirt were worn. There were wings attached to each shoulder, and both shoulders had a red shoulder-tab. The breeches were blue and worn with white gaiters, reaching to above the knee and buttoned on the outside.

Accoutrements

A blue belt with 4 bands of Royal lace was worn over the right shoulder. Around the neck was a blue belt edged in Royal lace, suspending the drum on the left thigh. A blue belt with 4 bands of Royal lace was worn around the waist with a frog of blue and Royal lace on the left hip, in which was carried the hanger or band sword.

Weapon. Band sword (Plate 92 D & E).

NOTE. The drum in the case of Royal regiments was a blue shell, ornamented on the front with the full Royal coat-of-arms. The hoops were red and roped with white ropes.

4. 21st Foot. Grenadier, 1751

Head Dress

The 'mitre' cap had a blue cloth front 12 in. high, edged in white tape. In the centre was a large embroidered thistle within a circle, on the outer edge of which was the motto *Nemo me impune lacessit*; the whole surmounted by a crown in heraldic colours. On each side of the circle there were embroidered leaves in white worsted. The front flap was red, edged in white tape, with the motto *Nec aspera terrent* along the edge, with the white horse of Hanover below. The headband at the back was of blue cloth and the top of red cloth, both embroidered in white worsted with leaves. On the top of the cap was a white-and-blue worsted tuft. At the back of the headband was a grenade with the regimental number, and on the band and back of the cap there were embroidered leaves and foliage.

Uniform

A red coat was worn with blue lapels, cuffs and turnbacks. The lapels were buttoned back to the waist and edged in regimental tape with button loops of the same. The coat, worn buttoned back, revealed the waistcoat of red, edged in regimental tape. The tape was white with a yellow centre line and a blue wave above. A red shoulder-tab was worn on the left shoulder, under which was located the crossbelt. The pocket flaps on both hips were edged in regimental-pattern tape. The skirts were buttoned back, revealing the blue skirt lining. The small collar was also edged in regimental tape. The cuffs were blue with a dip in the centre and edged with 2 rows of regimental tape, above which was a slashed panel in tape with 3 buttons. A white stock and shirt were worn. The breeches in the case of the 21st Foot, being a Royal regiment, were blue, with white gaiters reaching to above the knee, buttoned on the outside and supported below the knee with a black strap and buckle.

Accoutrements

Over the left shoulder a buff belt, 2¾ in. wide, was worn, buckling on the front with a brass buckle. Above this was worn the match case in brass. On the right hip and attached to the belt was a black pouch to hold grenades. Around the waist, but over the waistcoat in this order of dress, was a buff belt 2 in. wide, having attached, on the left side, a frog to hold the bayonet and hanger. Over this was a thinner belt in buff, holding a black ammunition pouch situated on the front.

Weapons. Musket (Plate 93 B), Bayonet (Plate 93 B), Hanger (Appendix 2, A).

5. 24th Foot. Grenadier, 1751
Head Dress

The grenadier or 'mitre' cap was worn by all Grenadier companies at this period. The 'mitre' cap for the 24th Foot had a green cloth front 12 in. high, edged in white tape. In the centre was the Royal cipher GR in white worsted, surmounted by a crown, in heraldic colours. Each side of the cipher was embroidered with leaves in white worsted. The front flap was of red cloth edged in white with the motto *Nec aspera terrent* and the white horse of Hanover underneath. The headband at the back was of green cloth and the top was of red cloth, both embroidered with leaves in white worsted. The regimental number also appeared on the headband, embroidered in worsted. At the top of the cap was a tassel in green and white worsted.

Uniform

The coat was of red cloth with green lapels, cuffs and turnbacks. The lapels were edged in regimental-pattern tape of white with a green line, and buttoned back to the waist. There were 3 button loops below this. The coat, when worn open, revealed the waistcoat beneath edged with regimental tape and with button loops of the same. A white stock and shirt was worn. A red shoulder-strap was worn on the left shoulder, under which was located the crossbelt. The coat was worn buttoned back to show the green facings and had a pocket on each hip, the flaps edged with regimental tape. The cuffs were large and of the face colour, dipping

in the centre and edged with 2 rows
of regimental tape. Above the cuff
was a slashed panel of regimental
tape with buttons. The breeches were
of red cloth, and white gaiters were
worn, reaching above the knee,
buttoning on the outside and held
with a black tape and buckle below
the knee. The turnbacks described
are green, although the 1758 Army
List states white turnbacks. Here
there appears to lie a discrepancy.
C. C. P. Lawson shows the facings as
white in his interpretation of Morier's
paintings whereas S. M. Milne in
Records of the 24th Regiment published in 1892 quotes them as willow
green. Milne goes on to say that
'Whether it is a mistake on his
(Morier's) part or whether the skirts
were now actually green will possibly
never be cleared up.' The plate in the
Regimental Records of the 24th
Regiment shows green skirts.

Accoutrements

Over the left shoulder was worn a
buff belt 2¾ in. wide and buckled in
the centre. A large black pouch was
carried on the right hip attached to
this belt. On the belt was a brass
match case with a chain to hold the
match for lighting the grenade fuse.
Around the waist, beneath the coat
but over the waistcoat, was a 2-in.
buff belt with a frog on the right hip
to hold the bayonet and hanger.
Over this belt was a smaller black
belt holding an ammunition pouch
in the centre.

Weapons. Musket (Plate 93 B),
Bayonet (Plate 93 B), Hanger (Appendix 2, A).

6. 40th Foot. Grenadier, 1751
Head Dress

The head dress worn by Grenadiers
of Foot Guards and Line regiments
was an embroidered cloth 'mitre' cap.
This name derived from the shape of
the head dress. The front was of
stiffened yellow cloth 12 in. high,
edged in white tape. In the centre
was an embroidered GR, surmounted
by a crown in heraldic colours. Each
side of the front was decorated with
white worsted leaf embroidery. The
front flap was of red cloth edged in
white, with the motto *Nec aspera
terrent* around the edge. Below this
was the white running horse of
Hanover on a red ground. The
headband at the back was of yellow
face cloth, embroidered with foliage,
regimental number and grenade. The
back of the cap was red, embroidered
in white. It was topped with a black-
and-white tuft.

Uniform

A red coat was worn, which in the
case of marching order, was buttoned
over and so hiding the panels of
regimental face colour and button
loops. The top was worn open and
buttoned back to reveal 2 small
pieces of yellow cloth and button
loops of white tape with a black
inner line and 2 gold outer lines
running through it. A red epaulette
was fitted on to the left shoulder to
hold the crossbelt. The coat was
buttoned back, revealing the yellow
face colour. On each hip was a
pocket flap edged in regimental-
pattern tape. The cuff was large with

117

a dip at the side and edged in tape. Above the cuff was a panel of regimental tape and 4 pewter buttons. A white stock and shirt were worn, these being revealed as the coat was turned back at the neck. The waist-coat worn under the coat was edged in regimental tape. Breeches were of the same cloth as the coat, and high white gaiters were worn, reaching to above the knee and buttoning on the outside. A small black tape tied beneath the knee on both gaiters.

Accoutrements

A 2¾-in. buff leather belt was worn over the left shoulder, with a large brass buckle on the front for adjust-ment. A brass match case with chain was fitted to the front, to hold the match with which to light the grenade. This belt held a large black leather pouch on the right hip for the carrying of grenades. A waist-belt 2 in. wide and buckled at the front was worn over the coat, with a black ammunition pouch on the centre front. On the left hip was attached a frog to hold a bayonet and short hanger.

Weapons. Musket (Plate 93 B), Bayonet (Plate 93 B), Hanger (Ap-pendix 2, A).

7. 41st Foot. Private, 1751

Head Dress

The head dress at this period was the tricorne hat. It was made of black felt, 3 of the sides being laced up to give the triangular shape. On the left side was a black cloth cockade. The top edge was bound with yellow worsted tape.

Uniform

The coat was of red cloth and very plain in appearance compared to those of other infantry regiments. It was single-breasted, bearing a pocket on each side with 4 buttons as ornaments. The cuffs were of blue cloth, ornamented with buttons. The turnbacks were lined in blue cloth and fastened with a button. The breeches were of blue cloth. Gaiters were above knee length, made of white cloth buttoned with black buttons on the outside. A white stock was worn.

Accoutrements

One crossbelt was worn over the left shoulder under the epaulette, which buckled in front with a large brass buckle and was attached to a plain black leather ammunition pouch. The waist-belt was 2 in. wide and buckled in front with a large brass buckle. Attached to this was a large frog which carried the bayonet and infantry hanger.

Weapons. Musket (Plate 93 B), Bayonet (Plate 93 B), Hanger (Plate 92 B).

Historical Note. The veterans were the 41st Foot, which in 1787 became an ordinary Line regiment. In 1831 it became the 41st or the Welch Regiment of Infantry, and in 1852 it was designated 41st (the Welch). In 1881 it became the 1st Battalion The Welch Regiment.

8. 42nd Foot. Grenadier, 1751

Head Dress

The head dress worn by the Grenadier company of the 42nd was a bearskin cap, whereas the rest of the Grenadiers of the Line regiments had embroidered 'mitre' caps. This cap was regulation for Highland regiment Grenadiers. Before its general introduction for all Grenadiers in 1768, 1 or 2 other regiments appear to have adopted them. The cap was mitre-shaped, the fur to be the blackest procurable and not over 5 in. in length, and was to be inclined towards the crown. The helmet plate affixed to the front of the head dress was a painted plate of red-painted copper, the raised part of the scroll edge and crown surmounting the GR being white. This may have been embroidered on red cloth like the other 'mitre' caps. The cap was lined in hessian cloth. No lines appear to have been worn as on the 1768 pattern of grenadier cap. A metal grenade was fixed at the back of the cap with the number 42 on it.

Uniform

The coat was of red cloth with an unusual turndown collar. Collar and cuffs were of buff. The coat was single-breasted with 10 buttonholes on each side of regimental tape, which was bastion-ended with a red line in the centre. The buttons were of plain pewter. The cuffs had a panel of 5 bastion-ended tape patterns with a button in the centre. The collar, cuffs and both edges of the coat were edged in regimental tape. Pockets edged in regimental tape

were situated on both hips, with buttons. The coat was squared at the back and shorter than the infantry coat of the period. A white stock and shirt frill appeared at the neck, as the coat was frequently worn open, revealing the waistcoat. The waistcoat was red, single-breasted and edged all round in regimental-pattern tape. The belted plaid was the kilt and plaid in one. The kilt was worn around the waist and the plaid hooked from the centre of the waist to the right and pinned or tied on the left shoulder, falling down behind the left arm. The belted plaid was of government pattern with the addition for Grenadiers of a red overstripe. The sporran was of plain brown leather with thongs and tassels at the front hanging down. The hose were red-and-white diamond pattern, tied beneath the knees with black tape terminating in bows.

Accoutrements

A black leather crossbelt was worn over the right shoulder with a frog fitting on the left hip to take the broadsword. The crossbelt had a brass buckle slide and tip for adjustment. A black leather waist-belt was worn under the coat but over the waistcoat, buckled in the centre with a brass buckle. This belt had a bayonet frog on the left front and an ammunition pouch on the right front. The ammunition pouch had GR surmounted by a crown affixed to the flap.

Weapons. Musket (Plate 93 B), Bayonet (Plate 93 B), Broadsword (Appendix 2, B).

Historical Note. The facing colours of the 42nd were changed to blue on 22 July 1758 by Special Royal Warrant, for their extraordinary courage and loyalty at the Battle of Ticonderoga. They were also given the title of 42nd or Royal Highland Regiment of Foot.

a General Officer's dress sword of the period.

Historical Note. This was the uniform worn by General Wolfe at the storming of the Heights of Abraham, Quebec, 1759.

9. General Wolfe, 1759

Head Dress

The tricorne hat was of plain black felt, round in shape, 3 sides were drawn up to the crown or laced up, giving the triangular appearance. A plain black silk rosette was worn on the left side.

Uniform

The coat was of scarlet cloth, very plain in appearance. The front was double-breasted with 2 rows of buttons, 8 buttons to a row. The top 2 buttons were left unfastened and the coat turned back. The cuffs were decorated with 2 strands of red cord with a button at the top of each. The trousers were of red cloth. The boots were of the pattern usually used for hunting. A white shirt and black stock were worn.

Accoutrements

A buff leather waist-belt was worn with a bayonet frog hanging down on the left side. Buff leather gloves were also worn.

Weapons. Officer's fusil and bayonet (Plate 93 D).

NOTE. The close-up shows the hilt of

10. Royal Artillery. Officer, 1760

Head Dress

A black felt hat was worn turned up on 3 sides to form a tricorne hat. The top edge of the hat was edged in gold lace. The front top was stiffened to give a dipped opening. On the left of the front at the top was a black silk bow with a gold lace loop and a gilt button which is thought to have been a gilt face, bone backed, with the design of a gun facing right with a pile of cannon balls. The button had a roped edge.

Uniform

A blue coat was worn with red collar, lapels, cuffs and turnbacks. The collar was worn turned down as shown and was edged in gold lace, as were the lapels, which reached to the waist. The lapels were buttoned back with gilt buttons, the button loops being plain twisted cord. The cuffs were round and had a slashed panel in blue, edged in gold lace, with 4 buttons and twisted cord loops. The turnbacks were red and buttoned back each side. A white stock and shirt were worn. The waistcoat was red and edged around the top, down the front and around the skirt in gold lace. It was single-breasted and buttoned down the front. There were 2 pocket flaps edged in lace with buttons below the waist on each side. A crimson sash was worn over the right shoulder and knotted on the left hip. The breeches were red, and cavalry-style black boots, with reinforced tops dipping at the back, were worn. A gilt gorget was worn at the neck.

Accoutrements

The sword belt was worn under the waistcoat, with a frog on the left hip in which the sword was carried.

Weapon Sword (Appendix 2, H).

11. 27th Foot. Grenadier, 1760

Head Dress

Being that of a Grenadier, the head dress worn was the embroidered cloth 'mitre' cap. The 'mitre' cap had a buff cloth front 12 in. high, edged in white tape. In the centre of the cap, instead of the normal GR, the 27th Foot Grenadiers were permitted to wear the badge of a castle with 3 turrets, St. George's colours flying, in a blue field and the name 'Inniskilling' above. This device was surmounted by a crown in heraldic colours. The front flap was red and edged in white with a border of red bearing the motto *Nec aspera terrent* in white letters along it. Below the motto, on a red ground, was a white running horse of Hanover. The headband at the back of the cap was of the facing colour of buff and had a grenade embroidered at the back in the centre, with the number of the regiment with scroll and foliage decorating the rest of the band. The tuft on top of the cap was white. The back of the cap was red with white embroidery of foliage.

Uniform

The red coat was worn with buff lapels, cuffs and turnbacks. The tape was of regimental pattern with a blue-and-red line and, although not sanctioned until the Clothing Warrant of 1768, appears to have been worn earlier instead of the tape authorised in 1742. The coat as shown was worn in marching order, buttoned up and with the top turned back, revealing the buff facing and button loops of regimental tape. The coat, by virtue of the lapels, was double-breasted at the top but turned into single-breasted at the waist. The skirts were turned back, revealing the buff lining and the red waistcoat edged in regimental tape. There was a pocket on both hips, the flaps edged in regimental tape. A red shoulder-strap was worn on the left shoulder, under which the crossbelt was located. On each shoulder was a wing epaulette edged with regimental tape. The cuffs were large and dipped in the centre, and edged with 2 rows of tape. Above the cuff was a slashed panel of tape with 4 buttons. The breeches were red, the gaiters buttoning on the outside, reaching above the knee and tying beneath the knee with black tape and buckle.

Accoutrements

A 2¾-in. buff belt was worn over the left shoulder and buckled on the front with a brass buckle. Above the buckle was a brass match case with chain to hold the match for lighting the grenade. On the right hip, supported by the belt, was a large black leather pouch to hold grenades. Around the waist and over the coat was a 2-in.-wide buff belt with a frog on the left hip to hold a bayonet and hanger. Over this was a black belt with ammunition pouch worn on the front.

Weapons. Musket (Plate 93 B), Bayonet (Plate 93 B), Hanger (Appendix 2, A).

NOTE. In the background is a Grenadier, shown wearing the skirts unbuttoned to form a full red coat.

12. 24th Foot. Grenadier, 1768

Head Dress

The head dress introduced in 1768 was the bearskin cap worn by all Grenadier Companies, rank and file, in the British Army. The cap was the same shape as the 'mitre' cap worn previous to 1768, but made of black fur. At the back was a red cloth patch and white cords and tassels, sometimes looped up behind and sometimes worn around the top, according to regimental custom. The helmet plate was of copper, the embossed parts being silver-plated and the back being black-japanned. In the centre of the plate was a crown surmounted by a lion, under which was a helm with the initials

G on the left and R on the right; above this was the scroll bearing the motto *Nec aspera terrent*. The cap lining was coarse hessian cloth. On the back of the cap was a silver grenade bearing the regimental number. The bottom edge of the cap was bound in leather.

Uniform

The coat was of red cloth which was lapelled, to the waist, in green cloth 3 in. wide, and fastened back by 10 pewter buttons, the buttonholes being taped in white. The collar was of green cloth and was sometimes known as a cape. It was buttoned down to the first button on the lapel. At the neck a black stock was worn. The small round cuffs were of green cloth, $3\frac{1}{2}$ in. deep, ornamented with 4 buttons and taped buttonholes. The skirts were turned back, lined in white cloth and held by a small grenade at the join. The back of the skirt was ornamented with slashed flapped pockets which were decorated with 4 buttons and taped buttonholes. The shoulders were ornamented with white tape passing across the top arm and had 3 horizontal white tapes. All tapes for this regiment had a red-and-green line running through them, the loops being square-headed. The waistcoat was of white cloth buttoned down the front to the waist. The trousers were of white cloth. Black gaiters were worn, reaching to above the knee and buttoning on the outside.

Accoutrements

The waist-belt was of white buff leather, fastened in front with a large brass buckle, the belt being 2 in. wide. Hanging from the left side was a large buff frog which held the hanger and the bayonet. Over the left shoulder was a buff leather crossbelt to which was attached a large black pouch used to carry ammunition, with a large brass GR and crown. On the buff crossbelt was a brass fitment to carry the fuse for lighting the grenades, known as a match case.

Weapons. Musket (Plate 93 C), Bayonet (Plate 93 C), Hanger (Plate 92 B).

13. 5th Foot.
Light Infantryman, 1771

Head Dress

The helmet, at this period, for the 5th Foot was peculiar to this regiment, although many variations were worn by other Light Infantry regiments. The helmet was made of leather with a turban at the headband in gosling green cloth (the facing colour of the 5th Foot). On the top of the crown was a metal comb with a red horsehair plume attached to it. On the front of the comb was a large lion with paws stretched out in front, the whole being in white metal. At the front of the helmet, where the peak joined the main body, was a large, upturned leather peak, edged all round in white metal. On this was carried the device of the regiment, in this case a large white-metal St. George and Dragon, with a scroll underneath bearing the title 'Light Infantry'. In the centre of the

scroll was a circle with a stringed bugle horn and the number 5 below.

Historical Note. This type of helmet was adopted by the Board of General Officers in March 1771, approving the design of Major-General Keppel.

Uniform

The light infantry coat at this period was much shorter than the usual infantry coat. It was made of red cloth, lapelled to the waist in gosling green cloth. The lapels were worn buttoned back, each buttonhole decorated with bastion-ended tape with a double red line running through it. The collar was of green cloth and also buttoned down. The buttonholes were decorated with regimental-pattern tape. Epaulettes were of red cloth, decorated with bastion and straight tape. The cuffs were in gosling green cloth, decorated with 3 buttons and regimental-pattern bastion-ended tape. The skirts at the back were turned back and lined in white, each skirt decorated with 4 'V's in regimental-pattern tape with a button at the apex of each 'V'. At the back of the waist, above the skirts, was a triangle in regimental-pattern tape. The waistcoat was of red cloth edged all round in regimental-pattern tape. There were 8 buttons down the front, each decorated with bastion tape. The breeches were of white buff, buttoning up on the outside to just above the knee. From the knee downwards, white stockings were worn, partly covered by grey gaiters shaped higher at the back of the calf than in front. These gaiters were fastened by means of pewter buttons on the outside.

Accoutrements

There were 4 cross straps in all, 2 over the left shoulder, carrying the powder horn and ammunition pouch, and 2 over the right shoulder, carrying a haversack and water-bottle. The waist-belt was of buff leather, 2 in. wide. Hanging from the left side was a frog, to carry the bayonet and a small axe. There was also another ammunition pouch, in black leather, which was worn on the waist-belt at the front. A large felt pack was worn on the back, fixed by means of 2 buff straps over both shoulders.

Weapons. Musket (Plate 93 D), Bayonet (Plate 93 D), Axe (Appendix 2, D).

14. 13th Foot. Drummer, 1771
Head Dress

The head dress worn by drums and fifes in the 13th Foot was a white fur cap. A white cap was worn by other regiments too, but the majority appear to have had the black fur cap in accordance with the Clothing Warrant of 1768, which states, 'The Drummers and Fifers to have Black Bear-skin caps.' The plate was white edged red and with the crown and Royal cipher. The number of the regiment was worn on the back. The cap was about 12 in. high, and the fur brushed upwards to a point at the top.

Uniform

The coat was yellow with red collar, cuffs and lapels. This was in accordance with the normal custom of reversed uniforms for Drums and Fifes and as stated in the Clothing Warrant of 1768, 'Those of all other regiments are to be of the colour of the facing of their regiments; faced and lapelled in Red.' The collar was open and the lapels edged and taped with tape and button loops. The pattern of the taping on the coats varied with different regiments; as the 1768 Clothing Warrant says, '. . . to be laced in such Manner as the Colonel shall think fit'. The waistcoat was white, as were the breeches. Black gaiters were worn, reaching to above the knee and buttoning on the outside edge.

Accoutrements

A white buff sword belt was worn around the waist with a frog on the left side for a band sword. A white buff belt was worn around the neck, and it held the drum on the left front.

Weapon. Band sword (Plate 92 D & E).

NOTE. The close-up shows a loop of regimental tape.

15. The Queen's Rangers,
1st American Regiment of
Canada. Rifleman, 1780
Head Dress

The 'mitre' cap had a black cloth front 12 in. high edged all round in white tape. In the centre was a crescent embroidered in white worsted. A black-and-white feather plume was worn on the left side.

Uniform

The coat was of green cloth, single-breasted, with 10 buttons down the front. The collar was rolled and turned down. The pointed cuffs were of blue cloth. Two slashed pocket flaps were worn at the front just above the waist, decorated with 3 buttons. The epaulettes were of interwoven chain. A white shirt and black stock was worn. The breeches were of buff leather and stopped just below the knee. White stockings and grey gaiters were worn.

Accoutrements

Two black leather crossbelts were worn, the one over the right shoulder carried a frog for the bayonet, and the one over the left shoulder carried the ammunition pouch. A haversack and powder flask were also worn, the former going over the right shoulder and the latter over the left shoulder.

Weapons. Musket and bayonet (Plate 93 D).

16. 87th Foot. Private, 1793

Head Dress

The head dress for this regiment, at this period, was very strange indeed. It was made of black felt and shaped like a very tall bowler hat, with a black fur crest worn fore and aft on the top. On the left side, at the headband, was a black cloth rosette

into which a green feather plume fitted.

Uniform

The coat was of red cloth and had short tails with green turnbacks behind. The front of the tunic was ornamented with a large panel of white tape decorated with 13 rows of buttons, 5 buttons in each row. The edge of the tape was scalloped. The collar was of green cloth, edged all round with scallop-edged white tape. The cuffs were of green cloth and pointed, ornamented with crow's-foot knots. A black stock was worn at the neck. Trousers were of green cloth, the inside and seat being of buff leather. Small black ankle boots were worn, with a black tassel in front.

Accoutrements

Two black leather crossbelts were worn, one on each shoulder. The one on the left shoulder was attached to the ammunition pouch, and the one on the right had a frog for the bayonet. A black canvas pack was worn on the back. The crossbelt plate, which held the 2 crossbelts together on the front, was of brass, engraved with the title 'The Prince of Wales' Irish' around the edge, and a harp with the Prince of Wales' feathers and a scroll bearing the motto 'Ich Dien' above.

Weapons. Musket (Plate 93 C), Bayonet (Plate 93 C).

17. 14th Foot. Private, 1794

Head Dress

The head dress worn by Battalion Companies of Infantry of the Line was the cocked hat worn across the head. The hat was turned up at the front and back. It was edged around the entire edge, both front and back, in white tape. A black rosette was fitted on the left side with a strand of tape and a regimental-pattern button. The button was pewter, with the number 14 in a French scroll with a dot at the opening. The plume was fitted behind the rosette and was black.

Uniform

The coat was red with buff collar, cuffs and lapels. The collar had a button loop of regimental-pattern tape which was white with a blue-and-red worm and buff stripe. The collar was open, revealing the stock and shirt frill. The coat lapels were buttoned back with buttons and button loops down them. The coat was fastened on the chest only with hooks and eyes, and sloped away towards the waist. The cuffs were round with buttons and button loops, in regimental tape. The turnbacks were white and fitted with a regimental device. On each side of the back were pocket flaps with buttons and button loops. A white waistcoat was worn underneath the coat. White breeches were worn and black gaiters, buttoning on the outside and reaching to just below the knee.

Accoutrements

Two white buff crossbelts were worn. The one over the left shoulder held the large black ammunition pouch on the right hip. The belt over the right shoulder terminated in a frog on the left hip in which the bayonet was carried. They were joined on the chest with an oval crossbelt plate of regimental pattern, which had the same design as that on the buttons. A canvas pack was worn on the back, in the centre of which was the number or badge of the regiment. The pack was worn on the shoulders with 2 white buff straps and a smaller connecting strap across the chest.

Weapons. Musket (Plate 93 C), Bayonet (Plate 93 C).

18. Royal Artillery. Gunner, 1797

Head Dress

The head dress at this period was the cocked hat, worn across the head. Complaints had been made that the cocked hat was too small, and an order in the General Officer Letter Book of 1790/4 stated that the depth of the crown was to be 14 in. and the remainder of the hat not less than 7 in. Across the turn-up at the front, and equally spaced, were 3 yellow tape loops. This had been introduced for the Foot Guards in 1790. On the left side was a black silk bow from which came the third tape loop. Behind the silk bow was fitted a white cut feather plume. The hat was bound in black tape. It superseded a hat of similar shape, worn in about 1792, which was without the loops on the front and edged in yellow tape.

Uniform

A blue coat was worn, with red collar, lapels and cuffs. The collar was high and opened at the front with 1 loop of yellow tape and a button on both sides. The buttons shown in the watercolour series by Edward Dayes are brass. The design was the Ordnance Arms in a shield, of 3 cannonballs across the top above 3 cannon (facing left as viewed), horizontally placed. The cuffs were round and had 4 buttons and button loops. The lapels were buttoned back with loops of yellow tape and buttons, and reached to the waist. A white waistcoat was worn beneath the coat, and a black stock and white shirt frill were revealed at the neck. Red shoulder-straps were worn. The turnbacks were white and fastened with a regimental device. There were 2 pocket flaps, 1 on each side, ornamented with 4 button loops and buttons. Above, and on each side of the centre vent, were 2 buttons above the back pleats. White breeches were worn buttoned at the knee, and black gaiters reaching to the knee.

Accoutrements

Two white buff crossbelts were worn, the one over the left shoulder suspending the ammunition pouch on the right hip. The ammunition pouch was white, in accordance with King's Orders of 1771. The pouch had a large flap on which was the badge of a crown with a semi-circular scroll beneath, with the words 'R.Artil.' and then the battalion number. This was mounted on a red cloth backing. On the crossbelt was fitted a red flask-cord which suspended a small horn above the pouch. On the chest were 2 white buff pockets for the hammer and prickers used for cleaning the vent. Over the right shoulder was the other white buff belt which suspended a bayonet frog on the left hip. This belt was fastened on the chest with an oval brass plate. The design was the Ordnance Arms in a shield, as on the buttons, with the words 'Royal' above and 'Artillery' beneath. The pack, when worn, was held by 2 white buff shoulder-straps and a smaller connecting strap across the chest. The pack, which is clearly shown in the watercolour of Edward Dayes, was of grey canvas with a circle in which the crown in heraldic colours was painted, above the letters R.A. Below this was the battalion number followed by the word 'Batt.'

Weapons. Musket (Plate 93 C), Bayonet (Plate 93 C).

19. 60th Foot. Private, 1800

Head Dress

The stove-pipe shako was introduced to the British Army by the General Order of 24 February 1800. It was made of black lacquered leather, measuring 7 in. in height, the diameter of the top being $6\frac{1}{2}$ in. On the front of the shako was a large stringed bugle horn in white metal. Above this was a black rosette, behind which a green plume was fixed. The caplines were of dark green plaited worsted cord and were fixed to each side of the shako and below the badge, with tassels, hanging down on the right-hand side. The peak was of black patent leather.

Uniform

The coat was of dark green cloth edged round the collar and cuff in red tape. The wing epaulettes were of dark green cloth and attached to the shoulders. The coat was single-breasted with a row of 10 buttons of regimental pattern down the front, the last button being worn under the waist-belt. The back of the coat had small false turnbacks lined in red, the centre of the skirts being slit to the waist with 2 buttons above, just below the waist-belt. The trousers were of white cloth, worn with small gaiters, the top edges of which were pointed, edged in black tape and decorated with a black tassel. A black stock was worn at the neck.

Accoutrements

One buff leather crossbelt was worn over the left shoulder, fixed to a black ammunition pouch. A red flask cord was fixed down the centre of the crossbelt which was fixed to a powder horn. A buff waist-belt was worn with a brass snake buckle. A buff frog hung down on the left side for the bayonet. The crossbelt plate shown was the pattern worn by the officers.

Weapons. Rifle (Plate 94 B), Bayonet (Plate 94 B).

20. Malta Light Infantry.
Private, 1800

Head Dress

The head dress was a black felt shako shaped like a top hat, with a black headband. A green feather was worn on the left side behind a black cloth rosette.

Uniform

The tunic was of green cloth with a plain red collar and cuffs. The epaulettes were of red cloth, ending in red worsted tufts. The tunic was single-breasted with 10 buttons down the front. The buttons were of metal covered in red cloth. The leading edge down the front was piped in red. A red sash was worn at the waist. The overalls were of brown buckskin, buttoned up to the knee on the outside with black buttons.

Accoutrements

Two black leather crossbelts were worn over the shoulders. The one passing over the right shoulder carried the frog for the sword. The one over the left shoulder carried the ammunition pouch.

Weapon. Musket (Plate 93 D), Hanger (Plate 92 B).

NOTE. In the background is a private in summer dress.

21. Bombay Grenadiers. Sepoy, 1800

Head Dress

The head dress worn was peculiar to Grenadiers of the army of the Honourable East India Company. The Bombay Presidency had its own army, as did the Presidencies of Bengal and Madras. The head dress was of the curious shape shown in the illustration. It had a wicker or leather frame on which was wound the pugri. Superimposed on this was a smaller version of the fur grenadier cap. On the front on a yellow ground were the arms of the Honourable East India Company. The head dress was decorated with a tuft on the top and tassels on the right side.

Uniform

A red coat was worn, similar in style to that worn by British infantry at the time. The collar, cuffs and lapels were yellow. The collar was high and open at the front, revealing a white shirt. The lapels were sewn back with button loops of regimental tape but without buttons. The coat, fastened by hooks and eyes at the top, sloping away to the waist. The epaulettes were edged in tape, with a worsted wing at the shoulder. A cord and tassel were worn on the right epaulette. The cuffs were round, with button loops but no buttons. The turnbacks were white. White shorts were worn, edged with blue lines, over which was worn a blue 'dhoti'. Sandals or slippers were worn.

Accoutrements

Two crossbelts were worn, the 1 over the left shoulder held the large black ammunition pouch on the right hip and the 1 over the right shoulder suspended the bayonet. In some cases belt plates were worn, but this was not always so.

Weapons. Musket (Plate 93 E), Bayonet (Plate 93 E).

NOTE. The close-up shows the 2 marks of the Honourable East India Company which were engraved on the muskets and bayonets. The smaller was stamped on the stocks. This mark denoted that the weapon was the property of the Honourable East India Company.

22. 56th Foot. Officer, 1801

Head Dress

The head dress was the cocked hat, worn across the head, the large back or fan being higher than the front or cock. The front top left had a black silk rosette, and a silver lace loop and silver regimental button, with the crown surmounting the number 56 with an open-topped wreath of leaves. On both ends of the hat were gold bullion hat pulls. Behind the rosette on the top was fitted a cut feather plume, coloured white over red.

Uniform

A scarlet coat was worn with cuffs, collar and lapels of regimental face colour, in the case of the 56th this was purple. The collar was high and open at the front, with a button loop of silver regimental lace and a button on each side. The jacket as shown was worn buttoned over so that the lapels of purple were underneath. The buttons were set in pairs. The cuffs were round, with 2 pairs of 2 button loops, in silver lace, with a button on each. The back of the skirts had white turnbacks which were held and ornamented at the bottom of the skirt by an embroidered regimental device. A slashed pocket flap was fitted on each side of the skirt, the flaps being decorated with 2 pairs of button loops and buttons. The centre vent at the top had a regimental-pattern button on each side. The epaulettes were silver lace straps with bullion tassels, and the number and type worn depended on rank. A crimson sash was worn around the waist, knotting on the left side and falling down. White kerseymere breeches were worn to below the knee, and black leather boots with reinforced tops were worn.

Accoutrements

A white buff crossbelt was worn over the right shoulder with a frog on the left hip in which to carry the sword. The belt was fastened on the chest with an oval silver belt plate, which had the design of 56 within a laurel wreath surmounted by a crown, and the honour GIBRALTAR below the wreath.

Weapon. Sword (Plate 91 H).

23. Honourable Artillery Company. Infantry Division, Private 1803

Head Dress

In common with the Artillery Division of the Honourable Artillery Company and with other volunteer units, the tarleton helmet was worn. The helmet had a black leather skull and peak, the peak being bound in white metal. A leopardskin turban was worn around the helmet, and the skull was surmounted by a bearskin crest. On the left side a white over red cut feather plume 14 in. long was fitted into a socket behind the turban. A band in white metal across the front above the peak bore the Company title. No chin scales were worn, but black tapes were fitted to tie the helmet on behind the queue.

Uniform

The coat was red with blue collar, cuffs and epaulettes. The collar was edged in white tape and worn open to reveal the stock. The coat was double-breasted. The skirts were turned back, revealing the white lining, and were ornamented on the back with a slashed pocket flap and 2 buttons above the centre vent at the waist. The cuffs were blue, edged on the top with white tape. The epaulettes were blue shoulder straps, edged in white and fringed in white cord on the shoulder. On the end was a device of 3 feathers in white embroidery. The breeches were white and buttoned at the knee, with black gaiters buttoned on the outside.

Accoutrements

A white buff crossbelt was worn over the left shoulder under the epaulettes and suspended a black ammunition box on the right hip. The belt had a green flask cord running along the centre. A waist-belt was worn, buckled with a Company-pattern buckle. On the left hip was a bayonet frog suspending the bayonet.

Weapons. Musket (Plate 93 C), Bayonet (Plate 93 C).

24. Duke of Cumberland's Sharpshooters. Rifleman, 1803

Head Dress

The stove-pipe shako was all in leather, tapering towards the top. The plume was of green feathers, coming from behind a black silk rosette. The caplines were of green twisted cord worn around the cap, with tassels hanging down on the left-hand side.

Uniform

The hussar-type jacket was in green cloth, single-breasted, the front being corded in green and decorated with 3 rows of buttons. The collar was of green cloth, edged all round in green cord and decorated with a stringed bugle horn. The cuffs were of green cloth and decorated with a crow's-foot knot in green cord. The bottom edge of the jacket was decorated with green cord, as were the back welts and seams, although the latter had the addition of crow's-foot knots. The tights were of green cloth, decorated on the front of the thighs with Austrian knots in green cord. Black gaiters were worn.

Accoutrements

A black waist-belt with a snake-buckle fastening was worn. The ammunition pouch was worn on the right side and the bayonet from a frog on the left. A green cord was worn over the left shoulder, attached to a powder flask, which was slung on the back. A green cord with a whistle was worn around the neck.

Weapons. Baker rifle (Plate 94 B), Bayonet (Plate 94 B).

25. 45th Foot. Officer, 1804

Head Dress

The hat worn by Battalion Company officers was the cocked hat of black felt, worn fore and aft, the fan and cock being of the same height and fastened together at the top with black tape. On the left side was a rosette in black silk with a loop of silver lace and a regimental-pattern button, which is thought to have been a flat silver button with the number 45 in a French scroll with a dot above. A plume normally worn was of cut feathers, being white over red for Battalion Company.

Uniform

A scarlet coat was worn, with the lapels, collar and cuffs of the regimental face colour (for the 45th this was green). The collar was high and open at the front, revealing the stock and shirt frill. On each side of the collar was a loop of silver lace with a button on the extremity. The coat in this instance was worn buttoned up, double-breasted, with the top buttons left undone and the lapel folded back to reveal the plain green lapels. The buttons were grouped in pairs. The cuffs were round and green, with 2 pairs of 2 button loops and regimental-pattern buttons. Silver lace epaulettes with silver fringes were worn, again depending on rank whether 1 or 2. The skirts were lined white, and this was revealed on the turnbacks, which had a bow ornament in silver lace at the bottom. There were 2 pockets at the waist, the flaps being decorated with 2 pairs of 2 button loops and buttons. At the waist were 2 buttons joined by a bar of silver lace. Below this was a further bar at the top of the centre vent. The buttons were at the top of the pleat. A crimson sash was worn tied around the waist and knotted on the left. White kerseymere breeches were worn and, as shown, were tied beneath the knee. Black boots with brown turned-down tops were worn.

Accoutrements

A white buff leather crossbelt was worn over the right shoulder, terminating in a frog for the sword on the left hip. This belt was joined on the chest with a belt plate of regimental pattern. The plate was oval and silver and the design of the number 45, in a convex circle with a ribbed edge. The edge of the belt plate was also ribbed.

Weapon. Sword (Plate 91 C).

26. Honourable Artillery Company, Artillery Division. Gunner, 1804

Head Dress

The helmet worn was known as the tarleton and was worn not only by cavalry but also by volunteers. The Honourable Artillery Company tarleton was similar to that worn by the Royal Horse Artillery, and was a black leather skull and peak surmounted by a large bearskin crest. The turban which surrounded the skull was of leopardskin. Above the peak was a brass band bearing the company title, the black stiffened peak being bound in brass. On the left side was attached a 14-in.-high white cut feather plume, and on the right side was a large silver Union badge device. The helmet had no chin scales, but had tape fitted on both sides and tied at the back under the queue. The helmet had a reinforcing strip on the left side to give added protection against sabre cuts.

Uniform

A dark blue double-breasted coat was worn with red collar, cuffs and turnbacks. The collar was open at the front in a 'V', revealing the black stock, and was edged in yellow tape. The cuffs were gauntlet-shaped and also edged in yellow tape. The coat was fastened with 11 brass buttons on both sides. The turnbacks were lined in red, edged in yellow tape, and the back of the coat was ornamented with 2 slanting pocket flaps edged in yellow tape and with buttons. Above the centre vent were 2 buttons and 3 rows of yellow tape, 1 down the centre and 1 on each side. The epaulettes were of red cloth edged in yellow tape with yellow twisted cord ends. On the epaulette was a motif of 3 feathers in white embroidery. White breeches were worn buttoned at the knee, and the black gaiters buttoned on the outside up to the knee.

Accoutrements

A white buff crossbelt was worn over the right shoulder, terminating in a frog for the hanger on the left hip. This was joined in the centre by a brass oval plate of Company pattern, as were the buttons.

Weapon. Sword (Plate 92 H).

NOTE. In the background is a cannon of the type used by the Artillery at this period.

27. Malta Military Artificers. Private, 1805

Head Dress

The stove-pipe shako was authorised for use in the British Army on 24 February 1800. It was made of black lacquered leather 7 in. high, with a plain flat top $5\frac{1}{2}$ in. across. The peak was also of leather. The plume was white and emerged from behind a rosette, above the shako plate. The plate was square in shape, the top being slightly scalloped. The design of the plate was probably the universal pattern plate, although they may have had their own particular pattern. The design of the universal plate was the Garter, bearing the motto *Honi soit qui mal y pense* with the Royal cipher in the centre surmounted by a crown with a trophy of arms and flags behind and a lion beneath.

Uniform

The coat was of blue cloth with black collar and cuffs. The collar was edged all round with yellow tape and was decorated with a regimental-pattern button and yellow tape button loops on both ends. The cuffs were edged at the top in yellow and decorated with 2 buttons and button loops in yellow tape. The coat was single-breasted with 8 buttons down the front, each buttonhole decorated with button loops in yellow tape with pointed ends. The shoulder cords were of yellow twisted cord, fastened to the shoulder by a regimental button. The tails of the coat were square-ended and edged in yellow tape from the waist down to the bottom edge of the tails. The trousers were of blue cloth and reached to just below the knee. Black gaiters were worn, fastening with buttons on the outside edge and a strap and buckle below the knee.

Accoutrements

One buff leather crossbelt was worn over the right shoulder under the shoulder cord, fastening on the front with a large brass buckle and slide. It hung on the left back hip with a buff frog at the end for the hanger.

Weapon. Hanger (Plate 92 B).

28. 12th Foot. Private, 1806

Head Dress

The stove-pipe shako was authorised on 24 February 1800, but was first mentioned in the Clothing Warrant of 18 February 1803. The shako was of lacquered leather, 7 in. high, the top being 6½ in. across. The plate was of stamped brass, 6 in. high and 4 in. across, and very square in appearance, except that the top and bottom were slightly indented. The design was of the Garter with the motto *Honi soi qui mal y pense* around the edge and the Royal cipher in the centre, the whole being surmounted by a crown. Behind the Garter on both sides was a trophy of arms and flags. Under the Garter was a lion. A white-over-red plume was worn.

Uniform

The coat was of red cloth, single-breasted, having 8 buttons in singles down the front, each button decorated with regimental-pattern tape with bastion ends. The collar was of yellow cloth edged all round in regimental-pattern tape. The cuffs were of yellow cloth taped across the top in regimental-pattern tape and decorated with regimental tape with bastion ends. The epaulettes were of yellow cloth edged in regimental-pattern tape and ending in white worsted tufts. The skirts were turned back and lined in white cloth. They were also decorated with slashed flaps, which were ornamented with buttons and regimental tape with bastion ends. Above the two centre pleats were two regimental-pattern buttons with a triangle of regimental-pattern tape in the centre. The trousers were of white cloth. From below the knee down, black gaiters were worn, fastening on the outside

of the calf with black buttons. The close-up shows the regimental-pattern bastion-ended tape.

Accoutrements

Two white buff leather crossbelts were worn, 1 over each shoulder, fixing on the chest with a crossbelt plate of regimental pattern. The crossbelt passing over the right shoulder carried a frog for the bayonet. The belt over the left shoulder carried the large black ammunition pouch.

Weapons. Musket (Plate 93 C), Bayonet (Plate 93 C).

29. 30th Foot. Private, 1806
Head Dress

The head dress worn was the stove-pipe shako introduced by General Orders of 24 December 1800. This shako was replaced by the one introduced on 20 October 1806 by Horse Guards Circular. The cap, as referred to, was of black lacquered leather, it was 7 in. high, the diameter of the top was 6½ in. and it was cylindrical. The plate was of stamped brass, measuring 6 in. × 4 in. Inside the Garter was the Royal cipher. The Garter was flanked on both sides by a trophy of arms and flags. Below this was a lion. On the top of the shako behind a black rosette was fitted a white-over-red plume.

Uniform

The coat was red, with collar and cuffs of regimental colour, in this case yellow. The collar was high and edged all round in regimental-pattern tape of white, with a blue line. The coat was single-breasted with 8 button loops at each side, of regimental bastion-ended tape. The cuffs were round with button loops and buttons. The buttons were pewter with the design of 30 in relief, surrounded by a full circle of leaves. The epaulettes had yellow straps edged in tape with a worsted tuft at the shoulder. The turnbacks were white, and the back of the skirts was ornamented with slashed flaps with button loops and bastions. Above the vent was a triangle of lace with a button on each side at the top of the pleats. The breeches were white, buttoned at the knee and worn with black gaiters which buttoned on the outside and reached to just below the knee.

Accoutrements

Two white buff crossbelts were worn. The one over the left shoulder suspended the black leather ammunition box on the right hip. The one over the right shoulder held the bayonet in a frog on the left hip. The belt plate was white metal with regimental design.

Weapons. Musket (Plate 93 C), Bayonet (Plate 93 C).

NOTE. In close-up is shown an officer's button of the period and a universal pattern stove-pipe shako plate.

30. 35th Foot. Officer, 1806

Head Dress

The head dress was a bicorne worn fore and aft with crimson and gold tassel hat pulls at each end. The hat was ornamented on the right side with 2 strands of silver lace from a cockade with a white-over-red plume of cut feathers. The silver lace strands were held by a regimental-pattern button in silver showing the number 35 inside an 8-pointed star. The hair was tied in a queue with a bow at the back.

Uniform

The coat was scarlet, double-breasted, and the tops turned back to reveal silver lace button loops and buttons grouped in pairs. The collar and cuffs were of orange, which was the regimental face colour. The coat could be worn in a variety of ways, buttoned back all the way down to reveal the facing colour of the lapels and the silver lace buttonholes or, as shown, for active service. In the latter case the silver lace extended from the lapels to reveal small buttonholes, when worn as shown. The collar was worn open to reveal the stock and shirt frill. The cuffs were plain round, of orange, with regimental lace and buttons. The epaulettes were silver, and the number worn, whether fringed or unfringed, depended on rank. The turnbacks were white, held at the bottom with a small silver embroidered ornament. There were 2 buttons at the waist at the back. There were 2 pocket flaps, 1 on each hip, with the regimental-pattern buttons grouped in pairs. A crimson sash was worn around the waist, knotted on the left front and over the shoulder-belt. White kerseymere breeches were worn which buttoned on the outer edge above the knee, and black gaiters, also buttoning on the outside edge.

Accoutrements

A white buff sword belt was worn over the right shoulder which terminated in a sword frog on the left hip. The belt plate joining the belt on the chest was a gilt oval with a silver circle with the word 'Sussex' surmounted by a crown with the number 35 in the centre.

Weapon. Sword (Plate 91 F).

NOTE. In the background is the rear view of a private of the Grenadier Company in marching order. Two white buff belts were worn, 1 over the left shoulder suspending the ammunition box on the right hip. In the case of the Grenadier Company this was ornamented with a brass grenade (Light Company having a bugle). The belt over the right shoulder ended in a frog on the left hip to hold the bayonet, obscured in the illustration by the haversack, and blue wood water-bottle, both worn over the right shoulder. The pack was yellow canvas held by 2 shoulder-straps, with a retaining strap connecting the shoulder-straps and fastened over the chest. A panel of face colour with the regimental design and number was painted in the centre of the pack. Sergeants wore the haversack and water-bottle on the right

hip with the belts over the left shoulder to leave the sword free, this being suspended on the left hip from a belt passing over the right shoulder. The other ranks' coat was much shorter and squarer at the bottom of the skirt. The overalls were white, buttoned with 6 buttons at the bottom, and were worn on active service at this period.

31. 14th Foot.
Officer, Light Company, 1807

Head Dress

The head dress was the stove-pipe shako, introduced in 1806. It was of black beaver with a black lacquered leather top. The peak was black lacquered leather. On the top centre was a black rosette, behind which fitted a green feather plume for Light Companies. On the front of the shako and in the centre was a silver-stringed bugle horn. The shako had been introduced by Horse Guards Circular of 20 October 1806. The shako differed from the 1800 pattern, as it tapered towards the top. The height was about 7 in.

Uniform

A scarlet coat was worn with buff collar and cuffs. The coat was double-breasted and, as shown in service order in the Peninsula, was buttoned over, so hiding the lapels which were also faced in buff cloth. The collar was tall, open at the front to reveal the neck stock and shirt frill, and had a button of regimental pattern and a strand of silver lace on each side. The button was silver with the number 14 in a French scroll with a dot at the opening. The cuffs were round and buff in colour, with 4 buttons and silver button loops. The turnbacks were white and held with a silver-embroidered regimental device. On each side of the skirts were slashed flaps with buttons and button loops. The epaulettes were of silver lace and of the wing pattern with bugle on each. A red sash of light company pattern was worn, the cords tying round and ending in 2 tassels hanging from the front. Blue grey overalls were worn, buttoning on the outside and lined with leather inside the legs and around the bottoms. These overalls were by no means regulation.

Accoutrements

The officer is wearing the black leather undress belt, from which hung the sword by means of 2 sword slings. A canvas pack and blanket were worn on the back and suspended on the shoulders with buff straps and a connecting strap across the chest.

Weapon. Sword (Plate 91 A).

NOTE. The close-up shows the cross-belt plate that would have been worn by officers when wearing the buff crossbelt. It was oblong silver with rounded corners and the number 14 in a spray of leaves.

32. 77th Foot. Drum Major, 1810
Head Dress

The head dress worn by the Drum Major of the 77th Foot was not

peculiar to the regiment and was a general design for Drum Majors. It was a bicorne hat worn across the head and richly ornamented round the top edge with feathers of red over white. In the centre of the hat at the top was a cut-feather plume of white over red.

Uniform

The uniform worn by the Drum Major and the fifes and drums shown in the background followed the general practice of reversed uniforms for the Corps of Drums; that was, instead of a scarlet coat with regimental face-colour collar and cuffs, the coat was of regimental face colour and the collar and cuffs were scarlet. In the 77th the yellow coat had scarlet collar, cuffs and plastron. The collar was open, revealing the black stock and shirt frill. The button of regimental pattern was silver (pewter for rank and file), with the design, on a slightly convex button, of 77, surmounted by a crown within a French scroll. The coat was single-breasted, hooking up in the centre, with lapels of silver lace terminating in buttons on the outer edges. Silver epaulettes had crescents and fringes. Around the waist was worn a crimson sash with a central stripe of yellow, being the face colour. (This distinction was abolished for sergeants in 1845.) The sash tied on the right hip. The back of the coat had white turnbacks and was ornamented with lace down the seams of the back of the jacket. The cuffs were scarlet with silver lace tapes and buttons. White kerseymere breeches were worn with black gaiters buttoning up the outside edge.

Accoutrements

A white buff crossbelt was worn over the right shoulder, terminating in a frog on the left hip and joined on the chest with a square silver belt plate, with a crown surmounting the number 77, pinned on. Over the left shoulder was worn a Drum Major's sash. It was of yellow cloth with a central silver lace line. On both outer edges was silver lace in a scallop design, the scallop facing inwards. On the chest was a silver plate into which were fitted 2 dark wood drumsticks with silver ends. The Drum Major's staff was normally of regimental pattern, in this case with a large silver ball at the top, richly engraved and decorated with regimental designs. The staff was criss-crossed with silver chain down to the ferrule at the bottom, where it terminated in 2 large silver flounders.

Weapon. Sword (Plate 91 C).

NOTE. In the background is a drummer-and-fife player of the regiment, in their bearskin caps. They wore the reversed coat with regimental-pattern tape and large wing epaulettes.

33. Bengal European Regiment. Private, 1811

Head Dress

The stove-pipe shako was introduced by the General Order of 24 February 1800. It was made of black lacquered leather, cylindrical in shape, measuring 7 in. high, the diameter of the top being $6\frac{1}{2}$ in. The design of the shako plate was probably the universal pattern, which consisted of the Garter belt bearing the motto *Honi soit qui mal y pense* with the Royal cipher in the centre, the whole surmounted by a crown. This design was flanked by trophies of arms and flags on each side, and a lion below. A black rosette was worn above the plate, with a white-over-red plume coming out from behind.

Uniform

The coat was of red cloth, single-breasted, the front buttoning with regimental-pattern buttons. The collar was of yellow cloth, edged all round in regimental tape. The epaulettes had tabs of yellow cloth, edged in regimental tape and ending in white worsted tufts. The cuffs were of yellow cloth, decorated with regimental-pattern buttons. The tails were turned back and lined in white. The skirts were decorated with slashed flap pockets, with buttons according to custom. The trousers were of white cloth.

Accoutrements

Two white buff leather crossbelts were worn, 1 over each shoulder, joined together on the chest by a crossbelt plate according to regimental custom. The crossbelt passed over the right shoulder and ended in a frog on the left hip, for the bayonet. The belt over the left shoulder was attached to a large black ammunition pouch.

Weapons. Musket (Plate 93 E), Bayonet (Plate 93 E).

34. 1st Foot Guards. Officer, 1812

Head Dress

A black beaver cocked hat was worn, bound all round the edge in gold lace. On the right side was a large black silk bow, a loop of gold lace and a regimental-pattern button. Behind the silk bow was fitted a white-over-red feather plume. The button of regimental pattern was gilt with a crown above resting on a GR cipher.

Uniform

A scarlet coat was worn with high collar open at the front to reveal the stock and shirt frills. The collar was blue, edged all round in gold lace. The cuffs were round and blue, edged with 2 rows of gold lace and with 3 buttons. The front of the coat had blue lapels edged all round in gold lace and had 8 gold loops and buttons on each side. The front fastened by means of hooks and eyes, and therefore formed a plastron front. The turnbacks were white kerseymere, edged in gold lace, and held with an embroidered device. On the back were 2 pocket flaps, 1 each side, edged all round in gold lace and with 3 gold lace button loops and buttons. The sash was crimson net and worn around the waist, knotting on the left side. The breeches were white kerseymere and white gaiters were worn, reaching to above the knee and buttoning on the outside. There was also a black strap below the knee. A gilt gorget was worn at the neck.

Accoutrements

A white buff crossbelt was worn over the right shoulder, terminating in a frog on the left hip, in which a sword was fitted. The belt plate was gilt, rectangular in shape, and, pinned on, was a crowned Garter with the Royal cipher in the centre.

Weapon. Sword (Plate 91 C).

NOTE. The officer is shown carrying the regimental or Union colour. In Line regiments the Union is the Sovereign's colour. The colour shown was 6 ft 6 in. × 6 ft and the staff 9 ft 10 in. long.

35. 42nd Foot. Sergeant, 1812

Head Dress

All ranks in Highland regiments wore the hummel bonnet at this period. It was of blue cloth with black ostrich feathers on the left side, which were drooped over on to the right side, giving the appearance of an all-feather bonnet worn at a later date. The headband consisted of 3 bands of red, white and green diced cloth. On the left side was a black cockade with a regimental-pattern button into which was attached the white-over-red plume. The bonnet had a detachable leather peak which was tied on with black tapes, the tapes hanging down at the back. The chinstrap was of black leather.

Uniform

The coat was of red cloth with a blue collar and cuffs and shoulder straps, the 42nd being the Royal Highland Regiment of Foot. It was single-breasted, with a high collar taped all round in plain white tape, only rank and file having regimental-pattern tape. The skirts were lined in white and turned back and edged in white tape. The Highland Regiments had the same pattern of skirt decoration as Flank companies of other regiments of the Line. The front had rows of bastion-ended tape, spaced evenly, with a regimental-pattern button in pewter. The button had the design of a plain circle with the number 42 in the centre. The cuffs had loops of bastion-ended tape with buttons. In the case of the rank and file, the tape had a red line running through it. The epaulettes were plain blue shoulder-straps, edged in white tape with a worsted tuft at the shoulder. The skirts of the coat had two slanting panels following the edge of the turnback, with 4 loops of bastion-ended tape with buttons. Above the centre vent and pleats was a triangle of tape with a button each side. The sash, normally worn around the waist by sergeants, was worn over the left shoulder in Highland regiments and knotted at the right hip. The ranking was 3 white tape chevrons on the right sleeve in the face colour (in this case blue). The kilt was worn and was of government pattern. Red-and-white hose and white spats were worn, the hose being tied below the knees with red garters and rosettes.

Accoutrements

Sergeants wore only one crossbelt in Battalion companies, which passed over the right shoulder and ended in a sword frog on the left hip. The crossbelt was fastened on the chest with a belt plate, which was brass and bore the design of 42 within an oval in the centre of a star of the Order of the Thistle. The pack was worn, consisting of a black canvas box-like construction with reinforced leather corners and with the regimental number and device painted in the centre. This was carried on the back with 2 white buff straps, 1 around each shoulder, and connected across the chest with a thinner white buff strap. The haversack and round water-bottle were carried on the right hip (the left, normally, for the rank and file) from straps from the left shoulder. A grey blanket was rolled and fastened to the top of the pack.

Weapons. Sword (Appendix 2, B), Spontoon (Appendix 2, C).

NOTE. In the background is a private of the Battalion Company with the full equipment of Infantry of the Line.

36. 7th Madras Light Infantry. Havildar, 1812

Head Dress

The head dress worn by native troops of the Honourable East India Company was of wicker or leather. The frame was covered with the pugri, which was wound round tightly.

Uniform

The coat was red, similar to that worn by British infantry. The collar and cuffs were of blue. In 1797 all Madras regiments were ordered blue facings. The collar was high and edged in white tape and it was open; a neck stock and shirt frill were shown at the neck. The coat was cut higher in the front than its British equivalent and had 6 rows of white tape. The cuffs were round with white tape button loops. The epaulettes were white wings with a blue centre and white fringe at the ends. A crimson waist-sash was worn. White shorts with blue lines around the leg were worn, over which was a 'dhoti'. Sandals or slippers were regulation.

Accoutrements

There were two white buff crossbelts, one over the left shoulder suspending on the right hip a large ammunition box. The other over the right shoulder held the bayonet in a frog on the left hip. A belt plate of regimental pattern was worn on the chest.

Weapons. Musket and bayonet (Plate 93 E).

NOTE. The close-up is of a socket of an India-pattern bayonet, showing the manner of marking. The markings are the Company's mark, denoting ownership and the maker, in this case J. Manton (of London) and the year, 1797.

37. Royal Artillery. Officer, 1815

Head Dress

The head dress worn by officers of the Royal Artillery was the 'Wellington' or 'Belgic' shako, introduced on 24 December 1811. The body and false front were of black beaver for officers and felt for other ranks. The false front was $8\frac{1}{2}$ in. high, the crown of the shako being about 6 in. high. The bottom of the shako was bound in black lace. A rosette was fitted on the left side of the shako, behind which a white cut feather plume was placed. Caplines were worn, fitted under the rosette on the left, looping down over the peak and hooking up on the opposite side. Two tassels hung at the end of the lines. The shako plate was a roughly oval ornamentally edged plate, surmounted by a crown. On the plate was a Garter with the words 'Royal. Regt. of Artillery' on it. Inside the Garter was the GR cipher. Below the Garter was a cannon or mortar. On each side, slightly above the cannon, were 2 flaming grenades, 1 each side of the bottom of the Garter. (A fuller description of this shako is given in Plate 43.)

Uniform

A blue coat was worn with red collar, cuffs and lapels. This pattern was worn only for a short time. The collar was open at the front, revealing the stock and shirt frill. On each side of the collar was a pointed loop of gold lace. The lapels as shown were buttoned back and the jacket fastened by hooks and eyes down the front. Each lapel had 10 bars of pointed-end lace extending nearly the full width of the lapel. On the outer end of each bar was a button of regimental pattern. The button was gilt with the design of a crowned Garter. On the Garter were the words 'Royal Regt. of Artillery'. Inside the Garter was the GR cipher. The cuffs were round and had 4 pointed-end button loops in gold lace and buttons. The turnbacks were red, as was the coat lining. The turnbacks were held by an embroidered device and on each side of the back were 2 pocket flaps. At the waist were 2 buttons each side of the centre vent. A crimson waist-sash was worn, tied around the waist and knotting on the left side. White kerseymere breeches were worn with hessian boots.

Accoutrements

A waist-belt was worn under the sash with 2 sword slings, 1 long and 1 short.

Weapon. Sword (Plate 91 C).

NOTE. In the background is a gunner of the same period.

38. Lieutenant-General, 1815
Head Dress

The large fore-and-aft cocked hat was of black beaver with gold-lace hat pulls at each end. The right side was decorated with gold-lace loops and a button. A red-and-white feather plume was worn on the top.

Uniform

The coat was of scarlet cloth, single-breasted, the front having 2 rows of buttons in 3s. The right-side buttons were decorated with gold-lace loops. The lapels were worn turned back, lined in blue and decorated with gold-lace loops. The collar was of blue cloth decorated with a lace loop and button. The cuffs were of blue cloth. The sleeves were decorated from the elbow to the cuff with buttons and gold-lace button loops, in a shallow 'V'-formation, in groups of 3. The epaulettes and aiguillettes were of plaited gold cord, the aiguillettes hooking up on the top 2 buttons, on the right front. The skirts were turned back and lined in white kerseymere. The skirts were decorated with buttons and gold-lace button loops, the loops again being a shallow 'V' with the buttons at the apex. A crimson waist-sash was worn, with tassels hanging down on the left side. The breeches were in white buckskin. Black boots were worn, the tops edged in gold lace and decorated with a gold-wire tassel.

Accoutrements

A white buff sword belt with brass buckle was worn, with sword slings hanging down on the left side.

Weapon. Sword (Plate 9).

39. 3rd Foot Guards. Sergeant, Light Company, 1815
Head Dress

The shako worn by the Foot Guards and Line regiments, except the 1st Foot Guards and Grenadier Companies, was the 'Belgic' or 'Wellington' shako, introduced on 24

November 1811. The shako was of black felt with a false front higher than the crown. The front was $8\frac{1}{2}$ in. high and bound with 1-in. black braid. The back was $6\frac{3}{8}$ in. and $5\frac{3}{4}$ in. at the sides. The bottom of the cap was bound in black braid, and the black lacquered leather peak was 2 in. deep. On the top left was a black silk cockade with a plain or regimental button in the middle. Behind this was fitted a plume (in the case of sergeants of Light Companies this was of green cut feathers). The cords or caplines were plaited gold cord, fitting under the rosette and hanging down on the peak and up to the opposite side of the shako. The 3rd Foot Guards had a regimental-pattern plate of a crown over an oval with baroque edge. In the centre was the badge of the Order of the Thistle. A light infantry bugle was worn on the left side below the cockade.

Uniform

A red coat was worn with blue collar and cuffs. The cuffs were edged in gold lace with 3 pointed button loops and regimental-pattern buttons. Down the front of the coat were 3 sets of 3-pointed gold-lace button loops and buttons. The epaulettes were gold fringed wings, of flank company pattern. The collar was high and edged in gold lace. On the back were 2 slashed pocket flaps with pointed gold button loops and buttons. Above the centre vent was a triangle of lace with a button each side, above the pleats. The turn-backs were white, edged in gold lace.

A crimson-and-blue sash was worn around the waist, knotting on the right side. Grey trousers were worn and, as shown, on active service were tucked into the grey gaiters, which buttoned on the outside. The buttons were gilt for sergeants with the Order of the Thistle upon them. Pewter buttons were worn by other ranks.

Accoutrements

Two buff crossbelts were worn. One, passing over the left shoulder, held the black ammunition box on the right hip; the other passed over the right shoulder and held the sword and bayonet. The sword and bayonet belt was joined on the chest with a belt plate. The belt plate was oval brass or gilt with the Order of the Thistle. The edge of the plate was beaded, the Garter motto and Thistle were separate and mounted over a green enamel oval. A large black canvas pack with reinforced leather top and corners was worn, suspended from the shoulder with 2 buff straps around the arms. A rolled blanket was carried on the pack. The haversack and water-bottle were slung on the left hip from straps running over the right shoulder.

Weapons. Musket (Plate 93 E), Bayonet (Plate 93 E), Sword (Plate 91 E).

NOTE. In the background is an officer of the Light Company in service order.

143

40. 3rd Foot Guards. Grenadier, 1815

Head Dress

The bearskin was 12 in. high, made of black-brown fur. On the front was a triangular brass plate, bearing the King's arms and the regimental title. Under the plate was a small leather peak, which was almost always hidden by the long fur. Gold caplines were worn, encircling the cap with tassels hanging on the right side. A small metal grenade was worn at the back of the bearskin, this being a legacy from the 1750s.

Uniform

The coat was of red cloth with blue collar and cuffs. The collar was laced all round with white tape. The blue cuffs were 3 in. deep, edged around the top with white tape and decorated with 3 white-taped button loops, each loop topped by a pewter button. The coat was single-breasted, fastening in front with 3 sets of buttons, 3 buttons in each set. These buttons were decorated with white-tape pointed button loops. The skirts were turned back and lined in white, having a slashed flap pocket on each side, decorated with 3 buttons and white button loops. The wing epaulettes were of scarlet cloth, decorated with tapes in the same pattern as on the front of the coat. The trousers were of white cloth. The gaiters also were of white cloth, reaching to above the knee and buttoning on the outside; they tied below the knee with black tape and buckles.

Accoutrements

Two white buff leather crossbelts were worn, one over each shoulder, fixing in front by means of a brass plate. The ammunition pouch was attached to the belt passing over the left shoulder, this belt being decorated with chain and match case, a relic from the 1750s. The bayonet was fitted into a frog on the belt passing over the right shoulder. The belt plate was a rectangular brass plate bearing the title and battle honours of the regiment. The close-up shows the pewter button worn by other ranks prior to 1790.

Weapons. Musket (Plate 93 E), Bayonet (Plate 93 E).

41. 7th Foot. Private, 1815

Head Dress

The head dress was the bearskin cap worn by Fusiliers and Grenadier companies of other regiments. The cap worn was introduced in 1802, being a new pattern from that previously worn. It was slightly smaller than the grenadier cap, which was 12 in. high, and approximately 9 in. tall. There was a brass sunrayed plate on the front with a grenade in the centre. Below the plate was a small lacquered leather peak. White worsted cord caplines encircled the cap and ended in tassels on the right side. A white plume was worn on the left side. On the back was a red cloth patch with a white worsted grenade.

Uniform

A red coat was worn with blue collar and cuffs. The collar was high, open at the front in a 'V' and edged all round in regimental-pattern tape, which was white with a central blue line. The front had 10 button loops of regimental lace each side and 10 pewter buttons of regimental pattern. The button had a crowned Garter, and in the centre was a rose, and in the middle of the rose the number 7. The cuffs were round with button loops and buttons. The turnbacks were white and edged in regimental tape. The back was decorated with slashed pocket flaps with button loops and buttons. At the waist, above the centre vent, was a triangle of tape with a button each side above the pleats. The epaulettes were wings with red straps edged in tape. The trousers were grey, and spats and boots were worn.

Accoutrements

Two white buff crossbelts were worn. The one over the left shoulder suspended the large black ammunition box on the right hip. A large brass grenade was fitted to the flap of the ammunition box. The belt over the right shoulder held the bayonet in a frog on the left hip. The belt was joined by a brass oval plate. The design of the plate was a crown over Garter, in which were the words 'Royal Fusiliers'. In the centre was a rose. The crown and Garter had starrays all around. This belt plate is shown in the illustration. The water-bottle and haversack were slung on the left hip. On the back the large pack was carried by 2 white buff shoulder-straps with a connecting strap across the chest. On the pack was carried a rolled blanket.

Weapons. Musket (Plate 93 E), Bayonet (Plate 93 E).

42. 30th Foot. Officer, 1815

Head Dress

The head dress was the 'Wellington' or 'Belgic' shako, introduced on 24 December 1811. It was of black beaver, with a false front edged in black lace. The false front was 8½ in. high and stepped down to 6 in. at the back. The peak was of black lacquered leather. The bottom of the shako was bound in black lace. On the top left was a black rosette with a button, sometimes of regimental pattern. Behind this rosette was fitted a white-over-red plume. The plate was a sort of oval, surmounted by a crown with a raised edge, indented in a baroque pattern. The caplines were crimson and gold-plaited cord which fitted under the rosette on the left, fell down over the peak and fastened up on the right. On the right, from the point of fastening, hung cords and 2 tassels. (A fuller description of this shako is given in Plate 43.)

Uniform

The coat was scarlet with yellow collar and cuffs. The lapels when worn back were of the face colour, but, as shown with the coat buttoned up, cannot be seen. The collar was high and open at the front to reveal the stock. On each side of the collar was a loop of silver lace and a regimental pattern button, which was flat silver with 30 within a circle. The coat had 10 buttons of regimental pattern on each side. The cuffs were round, with 4 silver-lace button loops and regimental-pattern buttons. The turnbacks were white kerseymere, held with an embroidered device. At the waist on both sides of the centre vent was a regimental-pattern button at the top of the pleats. There were 2 pocket flaps with lace and buttons on each skirt. A crimson sash was worn around the waist, knotting on the left. The epaulette (1 only in this case, denoting a junior officer) was silver, with silver crescent and tassels. The trousers were grey.

Accoutrements

A white buff crossbelt was worn over the right shoulder ending in a frog on the left hip, in which the sword was carried. The belt was joined on the chest with an oval silver belt plate of regimental design.

Weapon. Sword (Plate 91 C).

43. 33rd Foot. Pioneer, 1815

Head Dress

The shako worn by Line regiments was the 'Waterloo' or 'Wellington' shako, authorised on 24 December 1811. It was of black felt for rank and file, and black beaver for officers. The cap was cylindrical, bound round the lower edge with black tape, with a front higher than the crown of the shako. The high front was bound round the edge with black tape. The height of the false front was $8\frac{1}{2}$ in., the back and sides 6 in. and its crown measured about $6\frac{1}{2}$ in. across. Twisted white worsted cord lines were attached at each side of the shako and hung down the front above the black leather peak. On the left side was a black silk rosette with regimental or plain button. Behind the rosette fitted the plume, which was white over red for Battalion Company and green for Light Company. The cords and lines of the Light Company were in certain cases green cord and not white. On the front was worn a brass plate surmounted by a crown and in the centre a GR cipher. The plate was a curious shape of roughly oval design with indentations. The use of badges and numbers on the shako plate was permitted, by Horse Guards Circular of 14 February 1812, to those regiments entitled. In the cases where the badge or number was used the GR was slightly smaller. This order was further explained in the Clothing Regulations of 15 July 1812, which stated, 'Badges or inscriptions which Infantry regiments may be permitted to bear on their colours and appointments are to be worn on the soldiers' cap plate under the letters GR and regimental number or title placed under the badge or inscription.' A General Order of 28 December 1814 stated that, 'Corps of Rifles and Light Infantry and Rifle and Light Companies of regiments shall have a bugle horn with the number of the regiment below it, instead of a brass plate.'

General Order 291 of 10 August 1815 stated that, 'The cap, cockade and feather, plate and cap cover supplied every two years.' Another interesting piece of information was the 'non-approval' of an iron plate for the top of the shako. It was stated that, 'Iron in wet weather will rust and corrode felt and the object for which iron plate has been introduced, to preserve the head from sabre cuts, will be equally accomplished by the soldier carrying his forage cap in the vacancy of his regimental cap.' Obviously, the plate had been introduced and then cancelled, as it is further stated that the sum saved by leaving out iron plates was spent on oilskin covers to ensure the cap lasted the proposed time. The shako plate shown is that of the 33rd Foot.

Uniform

The coat was red and single-breasted, with a red collar and cuffs, in the case of the 33rd. The collar was high and open at the front in a 'V', and edged all round in regimental-pattern tape, which was white with a centre line of red. The tape on the coat was bastion-ended and set in pairs. The coat was loose-fitting, with round cuffs of red, and the skirts were lined white. The skirts were decorated with 2 pocket flaps with 2 pairs of 2 bastion-ended button loops with a regimental button at the bottom. The button was pewter with 33 in the centre of a continuous wreath. The skirt had a centre vent at the back, above which was a triangle of tape with a button on each side. The cuffs

had 2 pairs of 2 bastion-ended button loops, with a regimental button on them. The shoulder-tabs were red, edged in regimental tape, and with a white worsted tuft on the shoulder. The bastion-ended button loops on the chest were in 5 pairs of 2. The trousers were light grey, and worn over short black gaiters. In the case of pioneers a white buff apron was worn around the waist.

Accoutrements

Two buff crossbelts were worn, 1 over the left shoulder holding the black leather ammunition pouch and the other over the right shoulder holding the bayonet frog. These were joined on the chest with a regimental-pattern belt-plate. The black canvas pack, with leather-reinforced corners and top, was carried on the back, supported by 2 arm straps and a chest connecting strap. The water-bottle and haversack were worn over the right shoulder and hung on the left hip. The pioneers wore a black leather belt with a billhook in a sheath on the waist and a holster for the axehead, the shaft being worn across the back.

Weapons. Musket (Plate 93 E), Bayonet (Plate 93 E), Billhook (Appendix 2, E), Axe (Appendix 2, D).

NOTE. In the background is a private of the Battalion Company in full marching order.

44. 67th Foot. Officer, 1815
Head Dress

The 'Waterloo' or 'Wellington' shako was authorised for use in the British

Army on 24 December 1811. The height of the false front was $8\frac{1}{2}$ in., the back and sides 6 in. and it measured $6\frac{1}{2}$ in. across. Twisted gold and crimson cords were attached to both sides of the shako and above the black leather peak, with tassels hanging down on the right side. On the left side was a black silk rosette with either a plain or a regimental-pattern button in the centre. The helmet plate was roughly oval in shape, with indented and ribbed edges, surmounted by a crown. The design was of the Royal cipher GR and in certain cases with the regimental number underneath. A white-over-red plume was worn on the left side, emerging from behind the silk rosette. (A full description of this shako in Plate 43.)

Uniform

The coat was of scarlet cloth, double-breasted, with 2 rows of buttons down the front, grouped in pairs. The collar was of yellow cloth, decorated with 2 buttons and gold-lace button loops. The epaulette was of gold lace, decorated with a regimental device and ending in a gilt metal crescent and gold-lace fringe. The tails were turned back and lined in white kerseymere; they were also decorated with slashed flaps, each flap having 4 buttons and gold-lace loops. Two buttons were worn at the back at waist level. The trousers were of Oxford mixture. The close-up shows the pewter button of the other ranks.

Accoutrements

A crimson waist-sash was worn with tassels hanging down on the left side. A white buff crossbelt was worn over the right shoulder, ending in a sword frog hanging on the left side. The crossbelt was adorned by a crossbelt plate of regimental pattern.

Weapon. Sword (Plate 91 C).

NOTE. In the background is a private of the regiment in full marching order.

45. 69th Foot. Private, 1815
Head Dress

The 'Waterloo' shako was authorised for use in the British Army on 24 December 1811. It was made of black felt, $8\frac{1}{2}$ in. high in the front and stepped down to 6 in. at the back. A red and white plume was worn on the left side, emerging from behind a black cloth rosette. The caplines were of white worsted plaited cords, with tassels hanging down on the right side. The false front was edged all round with black tape. The peak was of black leather. The helmet plate was of an ornamented oval design, the edge being indented and ribbed. The design on the plate was the Royal cipher GR with the regimental number underneath. The illustration shows a private of the 69th Foot in marching order wearing the oilskin foul weather cover to protect the felt.

Uniform

The coat was of red cloth with a green collar and cuffs. The collar was edged all round in tape. The cuff was ornamented with 3 white-tape button loops and buttons. The coat was single-breasted with 6 pairs of 2-button loops and buttons. The regimental-pattern tape was white with a crimson, red and crimson lines, square-ended. The epaulettes were of green cloth, edged in white with a white tuft at the end. The tails were turned back on the outside edge, lined with white, with a vent in the centre. Above the vent was a triangle of regimental-pattern tape with 2 buttons each side of the base. The trousers were of grey cloth. Grey spats were worn.

Accoutrements

Two buff leather crossbelts were worn, 1 over each shoulder, held together on the chest by a belt plate. One carried the ammunition pouch on the right side, and the other the bayonet on the left. In addition to this a canvas haversack was worn on the left side and a water-bottle on the right. On the back a black canvas pack with a blanket strapped on the top was worn, by means of 2 buff straps going over and under the shoulder and a strap joining the 2 going across the chest. The crossbelt plate shown in close-up was that worn by officers at the time; it consisted of a gilt oval back plate decorated with a silver star with a gilt Garter and the regimental number in the centre.

Weapons. Musket (Plate 93 E), Bayonet (Plate 93 E).

46. 73rd Foot. Drummer, 1815

Head Dress

The shako worn by regiments of the Line was the 'Waterloo' or 'Wellington' shako authorised for use in the Army on 24 December 1811. It was made of black felt, the false front being $8\frac{1}{2}$ in. in height and the back and sides 6 in., the top measured $6\frac{1}{2}$ in. across. Twisted white worsted cords were worn attached to each side and above the peak of the shako, and tassels hung down on the right side. A black rosette was worn on the left side with a button in the centre. The helmet plate was brass, roughly oval in shape, the edges being indented and ribbed. The design on the plate was the Royal cipher GR. The whole plate was surmounted by a crown.

Uniform

The coat was of dark green cloth with red cloth collar, edged all round with regimental-pattern tape. The coat had 3 rows of buttons down the front, the 2 outer rows being at the ends of the button loops in regimental tape. The epaulettes were of green cloth decorated with regimental tape and had white tufted ends. The sleeves were decorated with rows of regimental tape in 'V' formation. The cuffs were of red cloth decorated with buttons and regimental tape with bastion ends. The skirts were decorated with slashed flaps with regimental tape and buttons. Two buttons were worn at the waist below the crimson waist-sash. The trousers were of Oxford mixture. The close-up shows the regimental-pattern lace.

Accoutrements

A waist-belt was worn under the crimson sash with a sword frog hanging down on the left side. The drummer's knee apron was worn over the right shoulder and strapped to the left leg. A buff drum sling was also worn over the right shoulder and attached to the drum, which hung on the left side.

Weapon. Sword (Plate 92 D & E).

47. 95th Foot. Private, 1815

Head Dress

The tapering stove-pipe shako worn by the 95th Foot was introduced in 1806. It was made of black felt 7 in. high. The peak was of black leather. A white metal stringed bugle horn was on the front, above which was a green plume. Green twisted cord lines were worn hooked up behind the plume and fixed to both sides of the cap, at the headband.

Uniform

The coat was of dark green cloth with black collar and cuffs. The Prussian collar and pointed cuffs were piped in white. The coat was single-breasted with 3 rows of buttons down the front, 10 buttons in each row. The short skirts were turned back and lined in black, the skirts being decorated with slashed panels with white metal buttons. Two buttons were worn at the waist below the belt, each side of the centre vent. The overalls were of grey cloth and some-times worn over the green trousers in battle order.

Accoutrements

The equipment was black leather. A wide waist-belt with white-metal snake fastening was worn with an ammunition pouch on the right side. Over the left shoulder was a black leather crossbelt suspending a pouch on the right hip. The belt had a flask cord running through it. Over the right shoulder was the strap holding the haversack. A frog on the belt held a bayonet on the left hip. The pack was carried on the back and suspended by 2 shoulder straps and a small connecting strap across the chest. A blanket, of white material in the case of the 95th, was rolled on the pack.

Weapons. Baker rifle (Plate 94 B), Bayonet (Plate 94 B).

48. Malta Fencible Artillery. Gunner, 1815

Head Dress

The shako worn at this period by the Malta Artillery was the second pattern stove pipe introduced in October 1806. The shako had a black felt body and a black lacquered top. It was 7 in. high, the diameter of the black lacquered leather top being $6\frac{1}{2}$ in. The peak was also of black lacquered leather. The badge appears to have been a plate, surmounted by a crown and possibly the words 'Malta Fencible Artillery' below the Royal cipher, and a cannon and cannonballs, as on the plates of the

Royal Artillery and Royal Marine Artillery. A white plume was worn in the top front of the shako.

Uniform

The coat was blue with red collar, cuffs and turnbacks. The skirts were lined in red. The coat was double-breasted and, as shown, had brass buttons in 2 rows up the front. The collar and cuffs were plain, although the collar appears to have had a tape-button loop and button, or a small grenade, at each side. The backs of the skirts had pocket flaps and buttons on both sides, and the skirts were held back with a grenade motif. The epaulettes were yellow worsted cords. The strap and crescent were of red cloth. The breeches were white cloth, buttoned at the knee, and were worn with black gaiters, buttoned on the outside and reaching to the knee.

Accoutrements

A white buff crossbelt was worn over the right shoulder with a brass rectangular regimental-pattern belt plate. This held a small hanger on the left hip in a frog. In full marching order 2 crossbelts were worn with bayonet and ammunition pouch.

Weapon. Sword (Plate 92 H).

NOTE. The close-up shows a cannon lock used on cannons at this period.

49. Malta Provisional Battalion. Officer, 1815

Head Dress

The head dress, worn in common with other infantry officers, was a cocked hat worn across the head. A plume was worn on the top left, the socket being hidden by a black silk rosette and a gold loop and button. On each end was a gold hat pull. The hat was of black felt and edged round in black braid.

Uniform

A scarlet coat was worn with green collar, cuffs and lapel. The collar was edged round in gold lace with a gold-lace loop and button on both sides. The coat had lapels in green, laced with gold button loops but could be worn fastened double-breasted, the turned back 'Butterfly' top revealing the lapels and lace. The cuffs were green and round, edged around the top in gold lace and with 3 button loops and buttons of regimental pattern. The skirts were lined white and the turnbacks were white with a pocket flap with gold-lace button loops and buttons. At the waist above the centre vent and at the top of the back pleats, were 2 buttons. The epaulettes were of gold lace straps with crescent and bullion fringes. A red sash was worn around the waist, knotting on the left side. White breeches and black gaiters were worn. A gilt gorget was worn at the neck.

Accoutrements

A white buff crossbelt was worn over the right shoulder, terminating in a frog on the left hip, in which the sword was carried. The belt was fastened on the chest with a gilt crossbelt plate of regimental pattern.

Weapon. Sword (Plate 91 C).

Historical Note. The officer shown is of the 2nd Battalion, the 1st Battalion had sky blue facings and silver lace. The two battalions amalgamated in 1806 and disbanded in 1815.

NOTE. The close-up shows a typical epaulette worn by infantry officers at this period.

50. West India Regiment. Private, 1815

Head Dress

The 'Waterloo' or 'Wellington' shako was authorised for the use of the Army on 24 December 1811. It was made of black felt, the front being $8\frac{1}{2}$ in. high and the back stepped down to 6 in. The false front and the headband was edged in black braid. The peak was of black leather. A white-over-red plume was worn on the left side, protruding from behind a black rosette which had a plain or regimental button in the centre. The caplines were of white plaited worsted cord hooked up on each side of the front with tassels hanging on the right side. The helmet plate was a brass oval, the edge being ribbed and indented, and it was surmounted by a crown. On the plate was a Royal cipher GR. (A full description of this shako is given in Plate 43.)

Uniform

The uniform was basically the same pattern as that worn by British Line regiments at the time, but with a few modifications. The coat was of red cloth with green collar and cuffs. The collar was edged all round in white worsted tape, and the cuffs were decorated with 3 pieces of white tape, each piece terminating in a button of regimental pattern. The front of the coat had false green lapels which were rounded off 3 in. above the waist. The coat had no buttons on the front, and it fastened with hooks and eyes on the inside edges. A black stock was worn at the neck. The short tails of the coat had turnbacks lined in white. The tails were decorated with slashed flap pockets. The epaulettes were of green cloth edged in white worsted tape and terminating in white worsted tufts. The trousers were of white cotton. The slippers were a privilege to the regiment, as the West Indians found it difficult to march in boots.

Accoutrements

Two buff leather crossbelts were worn, 1 over each shoulder, being fixed together on the centre of the chest by a regimental-pattern crossbelt plate. The ammunition pouch was attached to the crossbelt passing over the left shoulder. The crossbelt over the right shoulder had a white buff frog for the bayonet.

Weapons. Musket (Plate 93 E), Bayonet (Plate 93 E).

51. 71st Foot. Sergeant, 1816

Head Dress

The shako worn by the 71st Highland Regiment was adopted in 1806. It measured 7 in. in height and tapered in towards the top. It was made of black felt. The 71st wore this shako, but had their blue-grey woollen bonnets, with the diced border shrunk over the top. The black ribbons hung down behind. A bugle-horn badge was worn on the front.

Uniform

The coat was of red cloth with buff collar and cuffs. The collar was edged all round in plain white tape. The cuffs were square, 3 in. deep and decorated with 4 regimental buttons and loops. The coat was of standard single-breasted infantry pattern, buttoned and taped up the front. The skirts were turned back and lined in white. The tails were decorated with slashed flaps. Each flap had 4 buttons and loops. Two buttons were worn at the waist, with a triangle of lace in between. The wing epaulettes were of buff cloth, edged in white tape and decorated with tape, ending in white worsted tufts. The trousers were of grey cloth. The close-up shows the button of other ranks' at this period.

Accoutrements

Two crossbelts were worn, the one over the left shoulder suspending the large black leather ammunition pouch on the right hip. The belt over the right shoulder had the bayonet in a frog on the left hip. This belt was joined on the chest with a belt plate of regimental pattern. The water-bottle and haversack were worn on the left hip and the straps passed over the right shoulder. The large black pack was carried on the

back. The pack bore the regimental number in some cases and was held on the shoulders by 2 buff straps and a small connecting strap across the chest.

Weapons. Musket (Plate 93 E), Bayonet (Plate 93 E).

NOTE. In the background is a sergeant of the same regiment.

52. 21st Bengal Native Infantry. Havildar, 1819

Head Dress

A large bell-top-type head dress was worn in blue, with gold edging top and bottom and a diagonal line running left to right. On the top was a red tuft.

Uniform

A red coat was worn with yellow collar, cuff and lapels. The collar was high and open. The lapels were buttoned back and had buttons and twisted-cord button loops. The lapels stretched to the waist. The cuffs were round with 4 buttons and loops. A white shirt was worn beneath and could be seen, as the coat was worn hooked at the top but open and sloping away. The skirts were decorated with pocket flaps and buttons and loops. The epaulettes were yellow, edged white, with tufted wings. White tights or overalls were worn. Around the waist was a sash with a central stripe of the facing colour, in this case yellow. This was the same for sergeants in the British Army.

Accoutrements

A white buff crossbelt was worn over the right shoulder, terminating in a frog on the left hip, in which was carried a sword.

Weapon. Sword (Appendix 2, I).

NOTE. The crest of the East India Company is shown in close-up.

53. 2nd Foot Guards. Officer, 1821

Head Dress

The head dress worn, at this period, by the Foot Guards and Infantry was authorised on 22 August 1815 and worn until 1828. The shako was $7\frac{1}{2}$ in. high with an 11 in. diameter at the top and was of black beaver. The lacquered top was laced round with a 2-in. band of lace (in this case gold). The peak was of plain black lacquered leather. On the top front was a cockade with a gilt button, behind which was the socket for the plume. The plume, in the case of Battalion Companies, was white over red cut feathers 12 in. high. The gilt brass chin scales were attached on both sides with bosses and were worn up and tied behind the plume. Gold caplines looped the shako and came down the front below the badge, with flounders hanging down on the right-hand side. Other ranks' shakos followed a similar pattern, but were plainer. The badge worn on the front was a cut silver star with the insignia of the Order of the Garter in the centre.

Uniform

The scarlet cloth coat had a plastron front. It was double-breasted and worn in full dress. The plastron front was edged each side with gold lace and the front formed by bars of gold lace pointed at the end, leaving a blue diamond pattern down the centre. Gilt buttons were placed at the extremity of the plastron, being 6 in number on each side. The button bore the design of the Garter star. The cuffs were blue and edged in gold lace. The high collar, 3 in. deep, was edged all round in gold lace, and closed at the front. Prior to 1820 this had a 'V' opening to reveal the shirt frills. A white collar was worn and showed well above the collar of the coat. Epaulettes of gold lace, fringed, were worn. The number, whether 1 or 2, and whether fringed or not, depended on rank. The back of the tails were turned back, revealing the white lining, with gold lace along the edge and down the centre vent. The pocket flaps on each hip were edged in gold lace and had gilt buttons fixed beneath. The skirts were held back with an embroidered ornament on each side. A crimson sash was worn around the waist and knotted on the left hip. A gilt gorget was worn under the chin, attached to the collar of the uniform with blue silk ribbon and rosettes. The design on the gorget was normally the Crown and Royal cipher, but others had a full coat-of-arms and regimental name and number. The breeches in full dress were white kerseymere, and white gaiters, buttoned on the outside, were worn, stretching to above the knee. A dark blue silk ribbon was worn on each leg just below the knee and tied in a bow.

Accoutrements

A white buff crossbelt terminating in a sword frog was worn over the right shoulder, joining in the centre with a crossbelt plate. The sash was worn over the belt to keep it in place. The plate was gilt with a beaded edge, with a cut silver star and enamels of the Order of the Garter. The cross, in red enamel, had the oval with the motto pierced out of gilt on a blue enamel background.

Weapon. Sword (Plate 91 C).

54. 2nd Foot Guards. Officer, Grenadier Company, 1821

Head Dress

The bearskin cap worn by Grenadiers was about 16 in. high. A gilt plate was worn on the front bearing the King's arms. The gold cord caplines circled the cap once and had gold tassels hanging on the right side. A small black leather peak was worn. A plume of white hair 12 in. long was worn on the left side in a gilt grenade socket. This cap was worn by the Grenadier Regiment (1st Foot Guards, as it was called), and by Grenadier Officers of the Coldstream (2nd Foot Guards) and Scots (3rd Foot Guards). Gilt chin scales were fitted on each side of the cap.

Uniform

The coat was scarlet with blue collar, cuffs and lapels. The collar was 3 in. deep and laced around. The coat had blue lapels buttoned back. The lapels were laced around the edge; each lapel measured 3 in. wide at the top, 2 in. at the bottom and each had 10 buttons set in pairs. The cuffs were blue, round and 3 in. deep, and were circled at the top with an edging of lace. The skirt had white kerseymere turnbacks. The skirt flaps were edged all round in gold lace. There were 2 regimental-pattern buttons at the waist. There were 2 pocket flaps edged in lace on the back, with 4 buttons in pairs under each. A crimson sash 6 in. wide and 88 in. long tied around the waist, knotting on the left side. There were two 10-in. fringes at the end. Being a Grenadier Company officer, wing epaulettes were worn; the shoulder strap in gold lace was 6 in. long and 2 in. wide, with a crescent, below which was a scarlet cloth, wing edged in regimental lace and 2 rows of bullion, the outer one $1\frac{1}{2}$ in. long. On each was an embroidered Garter star below a grenade. The trousers were described as 'dark mixed'.

Accoutrements

A white buff crossbelt was worn over the right shoulder, terminating in a frog on the left hip in which the sword was carried. This belt was joined on the chest with an oval gilt belt plate of regimental pattern (shown in close-up). It was gilt matt finish, with a beaded edge. In the centre was the star of the Order of the Garter.

Weapon. Sword (Plate 91 A).

55. 91st Foot. Officer, Light Company, 1822

Head Dress

The Regency shako was of black beaver, $7\frac{1}{2}$ in. high, with a leather top sunk in $\frac{1}{2}$ in., being 11 in. in diameter. The top was laced round with a 2 in. band of gold lace. The bottom was edged in $\frac{1}{2}$-in. black braid. In the front was a large black silk rosette with a regimental button in the centre. A green plume was worn, emerging from behind the rosette. A large stringed bugle horn was worn on the front of the shako. The chin scales were of gilt brass backed with velvet, and attaching to the shako by plain roundels. The caplines were of green cord and were attached to the back of the cap, hanging down and attaching under the epaulettes, with the flounders hanging down in the front.

Uniform

The coat was of scarlet cloth with yellow facings. The Prussian collar was of yellow cloth 3 in. deep with a button and gold-lace loop at each end. The cuff was $3\frac{1}{2}$ in. deep, of yellow cloth and ornamented with 4 buttons and button loops. The coat was double-breasted with 2 rows of buttons down the front, 10 buttons in each row. The last button in each row was worn under the crimson waist-sash. The skirts were turned back, being lined in white kerseymere and decorated with 2 pleats and slashed flaps. The slashed flaps were ornamented with 4 buttons and loops. A button was worn at the waist on each side of the centre vent at the top of the pleats. The wing epaulettes were of gold lace, the straps being 5 in. long and decorated with a thistle and stringed bugle horn. The straps ended in 2 rows of bullion. The trousers were of a blue-grey cloth and were worn with half-Wellington boots.

Accoutrements

A white buff baldrick was worn over the right shoulder, held together in the middle of the chest by a crossbelt plate of regimental pattern. The belt was further decorated with a gilt chain and whistle. The baldrick hung down on the left side, ending in a sword frog. The crimson waist-sash went around the waist, with cords and tassels looping up and hanging on the left front. The crossbelt plate was of gilt brass, oblong in shape, with the design XCI surmounted by a crown, under which was a scroll bearing the title 'Argyllshire' below the number. For Light Companies a bugle horn was placed between the crown and the number. All the decoration on the plate was in silver.

Weapon. Sword (Plate 91 A).

NOTE. In close-up, is shown the wing epaulette that would have been worn by a Field Officer of the Light Company.

56. 77th Foot. Officer, 1823

Head Dress

The officer of the 77th in 1823 wore the Regency bell-top shako adopted in August 1815, but with the modifications, introduced in 1822, of height and of the abolition of the small back peak. The height was now 8½ in. and the top 11 in. across, the latter being of lacquered black leather. The body was of black beaver with a 2-in. band of silver lace for the 77th round the top and a narrower band around the bottom. The peak was of black lacquered leather. The chin scales were attached at both sides with bosses, and in this case fastened across the peak. The flounders and festoons in gold hung from both sides, and across the peak, the lines, encircled the cap at the back and ended in lines and flounders of silver, hooking up on a button on the right breast of the coat. The plume was white over red and of cut feathers 12 in. high, worn on the front top in a socket behind a black rosette with the regimental-pattern button in the centre. The button was silver with the design of 77 surmounted by the Prince of Wales' feathers, the whole in a French scroll. The badge, of regimental pattern in silver, was worn on the front.

Uniform

The coat was of scarlet cloth with a 3-in.-high collar with 2 loops and buttons at each end. Collar, cuffs and lapels were of the regimental face colour (yellow for the 77th). The lapels buttoned back on silver buttons in pairs, revealing the face colour, and hooked up down the centre to form a plastron. The buttonholes were twisted loops. The cuffs were 3½ in. deep with 2 pairs of 2 buttons and twisted loops on each. The turnbacks were of white kerseymere, held with a regimental-pattern skirt ornament. There were 2 buttons at the waist at the back above the pleats and centre vent. On each skirt was a slashed panel with 2 pairs of 2 regimental buttons and twisted loops. A crimson sash was worn around the waist, knotted on the left hip and over the crossbelt. The trousers were white. A gorget was worn at the neck engraved with the Royal arms. Silver epaulettes were worn.

Accoutrements

A white buff crossbelt was worn over the right shoulder, terminating in a sword frog on the left hip and joined on the chest by a belt plate. The plate was silver and bore the design of a crown, surmounting 77, pinned on.

Weapon. Sword (Plate 91 I).

NOTE. In the background is a private in parade order with the white festoon and lines on the shako. The other figure is a bugler of the Corps of Drums with reversed uniform.

57. Royal Artillery. Officer, 1828

Head Dress

The head dress worn by the officers of the Royal Artillery was authorised on 22 December 1828. The body was in black beaver, and the shako was about $6\frac{1}{4}$ in. high. The top was black lacquered leather and 11 in. in diameter. There was a band of black leather around the top and bottom of the shako. The peak was of black lacquered leather. There was a 'V' in black leather connecting the top and bottom band on each side of the shako. A white cut feather plume 8 in. high was worn on the top front in a large grenade plume holder. Gold cord caplines were worn around the shako and plaited. The plaited part fell down to above the peak and was fitted to both sides of the shako at the top. Cords and tassels hung down. The plate was a large rayed star, surmounted by a crown. On the plate in a circle were 3 guns. The chin scales were gilt brass backed with leather and velvet and worn as shown, tied up behind the plume.

Uniform

A blue coat was worn with red collar, cuffs and turnbacks. The coat was double-breasted with 2 rows of regimental-pattern buttons. The button was gilt with a crowned Garter. The Garter had the words 'Royal Regt. of Artillery' in it. In the centre was the GR cipher. The collar was high and embroidered with gold wire. The cuffs had a slashed blue panel with gold-lace loops and buttons of regimental pattern. The rest of the cuff was red. The skirt turnbacks were lined in red, on each side was a slashed panel ornamented with gold-lace button loops and

buttons of regimental pattern. At the waist of the back, and each side of the centre vent, was a button of regimental pattern. The epaulettes were gold-lace straps with crescents. Bullion tassels depended on rank. A crimson sash was worn around the waist. The trousers were light blue with a broad red stripe down the outer seam.

Accoutrements

A white buff crossbelt was worn over the right shoulder with 2 slings attached on the left hip. These slings were connected to the crossbelt in gilt brass rings joined with a short length of buff leather. The crossbelt was joined on the chest with a cross-belt plate of regimental pattern. It was rectangular in shape. The back plate was gilt, and frosted with a burnished edge. The device on the plate was a crowned Garter. In the Garter was the motto *Honi soit qui mal y pense* on a blue enamel ground. In the centre was a red cross in enamels, the quarters being white enamel. Below this in gilt was a thunderbolt.

Weapon. Sword (Plate 91 I).

58. Royal Sappers & Miners. Officer, 1832

Head Dress

The head dress worn by the officers of the Sappers & Miners was the standard cocked hat. The hat was worn fore and aft, and was higher on the left side (known as the fan) than the right side (known as the cock). The fan was 9½ in. high and the cock 7½ in. high. There were gold-bullion tassel pulls on the front and back, and the whole edge was bound with 2-in.-wide black silk binding. The cock was ornamented with regimental-pattern gold-lace loop with gilt button which, for the Sappers & Miners, was the Royal cipher within a crowned Garter inscribed 'Royal Sappers & Miners'. A white cut feather plume was worn from a socket behind the cock.

Uniform

A scarlet coatee was worn with a high blue collar edged in regimental-pattern gold lace. The cuffs were blue with a slashed panel on each, with 3 regimental-pattern buttons. The skirts were ornamented with turnbacks held by a small embroidered device; each tail had a slashed panel in gold lace. There were 2 buttons at the waist. A crimson silk net sash 6 in. wide and 88 in. long was tied around the waist, knotted on the left side and had 10-in. fringes at the end. A sword belt was worn over this. The epaulettes were gold-lace straps, 5 in. long and 2½ in. wide with a crescent, and had 2 rows of bullion tassels at the end, the outer row being 3 in. long. Ranking was displayed on the epaulette in silver embroidery. The trousers shown were of white duck.

Accoutrements

The sword was suspended from a gold lace waist-belt with 2 slings, 1 long and 1 short. The belt was fastened with a regimental-pattern buckle. The belt plate shown in the close-up was that adopted for other ranks in 1823. Before that date they had a brass buckle, except in the Gibraltar companies, who had worn a plate.

Weapon. Sword (Plate 91 I).

NOTE. In the background is an other rank of the Royal Sappers & Miners, in the bell-top shako adopted in 1830, with an 8-in. all-white plume. This shako was similar to the 1829 pattern, but without the festoon. The other ranks wore the belt plate previously described, and dark trousers with a red stripe down the outer seam.

59. 6th Foot. Private, 1832

Head Dress

The bell-top shako worn at this period was of black felt 6 in. high, the top covered in black leather 11 in. across and sunk ½ in. The sides were strengthened by leather straps in a 'V' formation. The chin scales were brass scales backed on leather. The helmet plate was a large brass star with a raised circle in the centre and the regimental number in the centre. This was surmounted by a crown, the whole plate being die-stamped in brass. The shako was topped by a white-over-red worsted pom-pom.

Uniform

The coatee was of red cloth with yellow collar and cuffs. The collar was edged all round with white tape and decorated with a tape loop on each side. The coatee was single-breasted with the buttons grouped in 5 sets of 2 buttons, decorated with white square button loops. The yellow cuffs were ornamented with a slashed flap with button loops and buttons. The coatee tails were turned back and lined in white, each tail decorated with slashed flaps and 2 sets of 2 buttons and loops. The epaulettes were of white worsted, the shoulder tabs being 5 in. long and of yellow cloth edged white, and ending in a worsted fringe. The trousers were of Oxford mixture.

Accoutrements

Two crossbelts were worn, 1 over each shoulder, fixed on the chest by a brass crossbelt plate. The belt over the left shoulder carried the ammunition pouch, and the belt over the right shoulder carried the bayonet frog. The canvas pack and blanket were worn by means of straps passing over and under both shoulders, with a strap attached to them going across the chest under the 2 crossbelts. The crossbelt plate was a rectangular brass plate bearing the badge and honours of the regiment. The button shown in close-up was that worn by the rank and file prior to 1840.

Weapons. Musket (Plate 93 E), Bayonet (Plate 93 E).

60. Rifle Brigade. Rifleman, 1832

Head Dress

The other ranks' bell-top shako was made of black felt 6¾ in. high. The top was covered in glazed leather and was 11 in. across. The leather top was sunk in ½ in. The sides of the shako were strengthened with 2 pieces of leather in the shape of a 'V'. The chinstrap was of black leather. The plume was black. The shako plate was a 7-pointed star, surmounted by a crown with regimental title and honours below. The shako plate for the Rifle Brigade at this period was all in bronze.

Uniform

The coatee was green with black collar and cuffs. The coatee was single-breasted, but had 3 rows of buttons forming a plastron on the front. The leading edge of the coatee was piped black. The cuffs were round with a slashed panel on each with 3 buttons. The buttons had the design of a crown with a bugle horn beneath; the strings of the bugle horn disappeared into the crown. Between the strings were the letters RB. The tails were short with centre vent and 2 buttons at the waist. The epaulettes were plain straps, shaped round at the ends, but with no tufts or tassels. The trousers were also green.

Accoutrements

The Rifle Brigade wore a black leather crossbelt over the left shoulder, suspending the large black ammunition box on the right hip. A waist-belt with white-metal snake fastening was worn with another large black pouch on the right front. On the belt at the left was a black leather frog, in which the bayonet was carried. A black canvas pack with reinforced leather top and corners was worn on the back by means of 2 straps about the arms, and held by a chest-connecting strap. The blanket and mess tin were fitted on the pack.

Weapons. Baker rifle (Plate 95 A), Bayonet (Plate 95 A).

NOTE. In close-up we show the button of other ranks' of the period.

61. 2nd Foot Guards.
Colour Sergeant, 1833

Head Dress

The 2nd Foot Guards had been renamed the Coldstream Fusilier Guards in 1831. This title, however, was never adopted, the word Fusilier being omitted. The only regiment previously to wear bearskin caps were the Grenadier Guards and Grenadier companies of the other 2 regiments. The large bearskin cap was 21 in. high and swelling out at the top. A large plate surmounted by a crown and carrying regimental distinctions was worn on the centre front a little way up, but was normally partially obscured by the long fur. There was also a small leather peak worn at the front, but again this was normally obscured. Two large bullion tassels were fitted to the right side, above which was fixed a red plume 12 in. long, in a socket. The chin scales

were fitted each side and tapered from wide at the sides to narrow under the chin.

Uniform

A red coatee was worn with a 3-in.-high Prussian collar. The collar and cuffs were blue. The collar had 2 wide bands of lace on both front edges, with a regimental button on each side. The cuffs were of blue cloth ornamented with a slashed panel with gold-lace button loops. The coat was double-breasted with 10 buttons in each row, the last 2 buttons of each row being hidden by the crimson waist-sash. The turnbacks were lined with white cloth and ornamented at the bottom with the regimental device. The skirts were also decorated with slashed flaps in gold lace with buttons on each loop. Two buttons were worn at the back by the waist, below the crimson sash. The epaulettes had a gold-lace strap 5 in. long with a brass crescent and bullion fringe at the end; on the strap appeared the regimental badge. The Colour Sergeant's chevrons were of gold lace decorated with the regimental colour, supported by crossed swords and surmounted by a crown. The trousers were of dark blue cloth with a red welt down the outside seam. The button shown in close-up is the pewter button of the other ranks', engraved with the Order of the Garter. Colour Sergeants had the same design but in brass.

Accoutrements

Two buff leather belts were worn 1 over each shoulder. The 1 over the left shoulder was attached to a large black ammunition pouch, and the 1 over the right shoulder had a fitment for the sword and bayonet. The 2 belts were held together in the centre by a gilt crossbelt plate on which was the Order of the Garter. A large black canvas pack was worn on the back, decorated with the badge of the regiment. On top of the pack was a large blanket. The pack and the roll were carried by means of buff leather straps, 2 going over and under the arms and a third strap passing over the chest under the crossbelts.

Weapons. Musket (Plate 95 D), Bayonet (Plate 95 D), Sword (Plate 91 D).

NOTE. In the background is a pioneer wearing a rolled blanket around his right shoulder and a white apron.

62. 13th Foot. Sergeant, 1833

Head Dress

This pattern of bell-top shako was authorised for the British Army by the Horse Guards Circular dated 2 July 1830. It was made of black felt, 6 in. high with a glazed leather top 11 in. across and sunk in $\frac{1}{2}$ in. The sides of the shako were strengthened by 2 pieces of leather in a 'V' formation on each side. A green worsted ball in a brass socket was worn on the top front of the shako. The helmet plate was die-stamped in brass. The design was of a 7-pointed rayed star, surmounted by a crown. In the centre was a circle with the number 13 in the middle. The chin scales were of brass.

Uniform

The coatee was of red cloth, single-breasted, buttoned and taped down the front. The collar was of yellow cloth, edged all round in white tape and decorated with a button loop, also in white tape. The cuffs were 3 in. deep and decorated with a slashed flap ornamented with white tape and regimental-pattern buttons. Two buttons were worn at the back, below the crimson waist-sash. The straps of the epaulettes were of yellow cloth, edged in white tape, and ending in white worsted tufts. The trousers were of white cloth. The design of the button shown in the close-up was the same as worn by officers and other ranks.

Accoutrements

Two buff leather crossbelts were worn, 1 over each shoulder, fixed on the chest by a crossbelt plate of regimental pattern. The belt over the left shoulder carried the large black ammunition pouch. The belt over the right shoulder carried a frog for the sword and bayonet.

Weapons. Musket (Plate 95 D), Bayonet (Plate 95 D), Sword (Plate 91 I).

63. 1st Foot Guards. Officer, 1834

Head Dress

The head dress worn by all Foot Guards was the bearskin cap, introduced into the 2nd and 3rd in 1831. The cap was of black bearskin and

21 in. high, swelling and shaped at the top. A large sun-rayed plate was worn on the front with a large gilt grenade. A small black lacquered leather peak was fitted at the front. Two large bullion tassels were fitted on the right side and a white plume on the left. The chinchain was gilt brass interlocking rings backed with leather and velvet. It was fitted on both sides of the cap and tapered from wide at the sides to narrow under the chin.

Uniform

A scarlet coatee was worn with blue collar and cuffs. The collar was 3 in. high and closed at the front. On each side was a panel of gold embroidery, each with a silver grenade. The coatee was double-breasted with gilt buttons of regimental pattern. The buttons were gilt with the design of a crown and Garter with the Royal cipher reversed and intertwined. The epaulettes were gold-lace straps with bullion tassels and a silver grenade. The cuffs were round with a slashed panel ornamented with 4 gold-lace button loops of regimental pattern. The skirts were lined white with false white turnbacks with an embroidered grenade. On each side were 4 panels of embroidered lace with buttons in a slashed panel. A crimson waist-sash was worn, knotting on the left hip and falling. White trousers were worn in summer.

Accoutrements

A white buff crossbelt was worn over the right shoulder and held on the chest with a belt plate. The belt had a frog on the left hip from which was suspended the sword. The plate was gilt frosted and rectangular. In the centre was a gilt grenade with the Royal cipher and crown on the bomb. The cipher was intertwined. The belt plate, shown in close-up, was that worn between 1837 and 1855.

Weapon. Sword (Plate 91 I).

NOTE. In the background is an officer with the trousers worn in winter, of dark mixture with a gold-lace stripe.

64. 3rd Foot Guards. Colour Sergeant, 1834
Head Dress

The bearskin cap was 21 in. high and made of black fur, swelling out at the top. A large plate, surmounted by a crown bearing the regimental honours and distinctions, was worn on the front. There was also a leather peak on the front. The helmet plate and peak were normally obscured by the long fur. Two large bullion tassels were fixed to the right side. The chinchain was of brass interlocking rings backed with leather; the chain was tapered, being wide at the sides and narrow under the chin.

Uniform

The short-tailed coatee was of red cloth with a 3-in.-high Prussian collar. The collar and cuffs were of blue cloth. The collar was ornamented with 2 wide pieces of gold lace on both front edges and decorated with a regimental button on each side. The cuffs had a slashed panel ornamented with gold-lace button loops and buttons. The coatee was double-breasted, with 2 rows of gilt buttons down the front, 9 buttons in each row. The last button in each row was worn under the crimson waist-sash. The turnbacks were lined in white cloth and ornamented at the bottom by the regimental device. Two regimental buttons were worn at the waist below the crimson sash. The skirts were ornamented with a slashed panel on both sides with gold lace and regimental buttons. The epaulettes had a gold lace strap 5 in. long and $2\frac{1}{2}$ in. wide with a regimental crescent at the end in brass, then fringed with bullion lace. The Colour Sergeant's chevrons were of gold lace with the regimental colour above, supported by two scimitars, the colour surmounted by a crown. The trousers were of white cloth. The regimental button was brass, the design being the Order of the Thistle.

Accoutrements

Two white buff leather crossbelts were worn, 1 over each shoulder, fixed together on the front by a crossbelt plate. The belt passing over the left shoulder carried a large black ammunition pouch, and the belt over the right shoulder ended in a frog which carried the bayonet and the sword. The belt plate shown was worn by officers and Colour Sergeants. It consisted of a gilt frosted plate, mounted with a white-metal star in the centre and a thistle surrounded by a Garter bearing the motto *Nemo me impune lacessit*.

The thistle was backed with green enamels.

Weapons. Musket (Plate 95 D), Bayonet (Plate 95 D), Sword (Plate 91 E).

Historical Note. The 3rd Foot Guards had been renamed, in 1831, the Scots Fusilier Guards. This title was used by them until 1877.

65. Rifle Brigade. Officer, 1834
Head Dress

The head dress worn was the bell-top shako introduced by Horse Guards Circular of 2 July 1830. It was belled out towards the top, and the body was of black beaver for officers and black felt for other ranks. The shako was 6 in. high and the sunken black, glazed leather top was 11 in. across. The top and bottom were bound with a band of black lacquered leather. The shako was supported on both sides with a broad 'V' in black lacquered leather, with the wider part at the top, and the 'V' connecting the top and bottom band. The peak at the front was of black lacquered leather. The cap had a dark green cord festoon fixed at the top on the left, falling on the peak and hooking up on the right. Lines encircled the cap, came down on the right of the cap and attached to the jacket. It is interesting to note that the Rifle Brigade wore festoons, whereas these had been discontinued, in 1830, for regiments of the Line. The chin scales were bronzed and fitted at both sides with a circular boss with a stringed bugle horn in the centre. A green ball tuft was worn, although infantry of the Line still retained a cut feather plume. The sergeant in the background, however, wears a falling plume in green. A large bronze star plate surmounted by a crown was worn on the front with the Brigade badge and battle honours. Later, in 1834, the festoons and lines were discontinued.

Uniform

The jacket worn at this period by the Rifle Brigade was a shell jacket on the hussar pattern but in dark green, which later was made much darker owing to the problem of the cloth fading. The jacket collar and cuffs were entirely of green cloth, the collar being 3 in. high; it was laced round with black regimental lace and ornamented with black russia braid. The jacket was single-breasted, with 5 rows of black metal buttons, and trimmed with black cord loops, extending the full width of the jacket at the top and about 6 in. at the bottom. The loops were intersected with black russia braid. The sleeve was pointed, 3 in. deep, laced round with black lace and ornamented up the sleeve, depending on rank, with russia braid. The edges of the jacket were edged and ornamented in black lace which passed over the knots at the back and up the welts. The side seams were also richly decorated with russia braid. A pelisse was worn by officers, this also being of green cloth, and ornamented in a similar manner to the jacket, with the addition of a 4-in.-deep fur collar and 3-in.-deep fur cuff. The rest of the pelisse was edged with fur, with an inlet into the sleeve and welts. This was worn with black cord neck lines with slides and acorn ends. The overalls were of green cloth. A crimson barrel sash was worn around the waist and knotted at the back with cord and tassels, coming round to hook up at the front waist.

Accoutrements

A black, lacquered or patent leather belt and pouch, was worn over the left shoulder. Mounted on the front was a silver lionhead, with a chain attached to a whistle. Between the lionhead and whistle was placed the Brigade badge in silver. On the pouch was a bugle horn, stringed. A thin sword belt with silver snake fastener was worn around the hip with 5 slings, 2 for the sword (1 long and 1 short) and 3 for the plain, black patent leather sabretache.

Weapon. Sword (Plate 91 I). In the Rifles the hilt was silver with a bugle horn in lieu of Royal Cipher.

NOTE. In the background is a sergeant who also wore the crossbelt, similar to that of the officer, and a crimson sash.

66. 23rd Foot. Sergeant, 1835

Head Dress

The black fur bearskin was worn by all Fusiliers at this period. The bearskin was 21 in. high with tapering brass chin scales fixed on each side. The peak was of black patent leather. The brass triangular helmet plate was decorated with sunrays, each ray having a regimental honour or distinction on it. In the centre of the plate was a large grenade with the Prince of Wales' feathers in the centre, surrounded by a Garter bearing the title 'Royal Welch Fusiliers'. At the end of 1835 the brass plate and leather peak were discontinued.

Uniform

The coatee was of red cloth with blue collar and cuffs. The collar was edged all round with white tape and decorated with open-bastion tape. The cuffs were ornamented with slashed flaps and 3 buttons. The coatee was single-breasted with 8 buttons down the front, decorated with button loops in open-bastion tape. A red sash was worn at the waist. The epaulettes were of red cloth, decorated with white tape, and had white worsted tufts at the end. The coatee tails were turned back and edged in white. The tails were decorated with slashed panels, ornamented with buttons and button loops in bastion tape. Two buttons were worn at the waist, below the red sash. The trousers were of dark blue cloth with a red welt down the outside seam.

Accoutrements

Two white, buff leather crossbelts were worn, held together on the chest by a crossbelt plate. The belt over the right shoulder carried the frog for the bayonet and the sword, and the one over the left shoulder carried the ammunition pouch. The crossbelt plate shown in close-up was the pattern worn by sergeants. It was a gilt rectangular plate with a grenade in the centre, bearing the Prince of Wales' feathers and the regimental title.

Weapons. Musket (Plate 95 D), Bayonet (Plate 95 D), Sword (Plate 91 I).

67. 2nd Foot Guards. Negro Bandsman, 1836

Head Dress

A white turban was worn decorated with silver chains. The headband was of gold lace, edged in red cord. On the top of the white turban was a red patch decorated with a gilt crescent. The red plume came out from the centre of the crescent. A gilt badge of regimental pattern was worn on the front of the turban.

Uniform

The coatee was of scarlet cloth with blue collar and cuffs. The collar was decorated with gold lace and the regimental badge. The cuffs were decorated with slashed flaps with gold lace with a regimental button in the centre of each loop, the loopings being in pairs with a red light in the centre. The coatee was single-breasted, with 3 rows of buttons down the front in pairs, 8 buttons in each row decorated with gold-lace button loops. The sleeves of the coatee were red down to the elbow, and from there to the edge of the cuff were white. The sleeves were decorated with 6 upturned 'V's in gold lace. The skirts were turned back and lined in white and decorated with a slashed flap with 4 buttons and loops, being in pairs. Two buttons were worn above the skirts on each side of the centre vent. The epaulettes were of blue cloth edged in gold lace, the boards being 5 in. long and ending in a gilt crescent with a regimental badge in the centre. The trousers were of white cloth.

Accoutrements

A white buff waist-belt was worn under the coatee with a sword frog hanging down on the left side. The instrument in the illustration was known as a 'Jingling Johnnie'.

Weapon. Sword (Plate 92 D & E).

68. Royal Artillery. Officer, 1840

Head Dress

The head dress was the bell-top shako that had been authorised on 27 August 1835. The body of the shako was of black beaver, 6 in. high, and the top was 11 in. in diameter. The top was of black lacquered leather. A band of leather around the bottom and top of the shako was connected on both sides with 2 bands of leather sewn on the body in a 'V' shape. These bands on each side added support to the shako. The peak was of black lacquered leather. A black leather chinstrap was worn. A white feather plume was fitted in a grenade-shaped holder at the top front of the shako. On the bomb of the grenade was the Royal cipher. The shako plate was gilt and the design was a diamante star surmounted by a crown. On the star in the centre was a field gun with a scroll beneath, with the word *Ubique*. The plate measured about 5 in. in height.

Uniform

A blue coatee was worn with red collar and cuffs. The coatee was double-breasted and fastened with gilt buttons. The design was gilt with a 6-scalloped edge. In the centre was a crown above 3 guns, placed 1 above the other. The cuffs were round with a slashed panel on each. The panel had 3 buttons, and it was heavily embroidered. The collar was red, 3 in. high and closed at the front. There was a grenade each side, and the rest of the collar was heavily embroidered. The epaulettes were gold-lace straps with crescents and bullion tassels; on each epaulette was a large silver embroidered grenade. A crimson net waist-sash was worn around the waist and knotted on the left side. White trousers were worn in summer.

Accoutrements

Over the right shoulder a white buff crossbelt was worn which terminated in a frog on the left hip. The belt was joined on the chest with a crossbelt plate. The plate was gilt, the background was frosted. On the plate was pinned a crowned Garter with the Royal arms in the centre. On both sides of the Garter there were sprays of roses, shamrocks and thistles. Below the Garter and covering the bottom of both branches of the spray was a scroll with the word *Ubique*. Below the scroll was a field gun, and another scroll under the gun with the words *Quo fas et gloria ducunt*. Other ranks wore the same, but die-stamped.

Weapon. Sword (Plate 91 I).

NOTE. The close-up in this plate shows the button described above.

69. 24th Foot. Private, 1840

Head Dress

All infantry at this period had the bell-top shako which was authorised on 27 August 1835. The body was made of black felt 6 in. high, the top being covered in black leather 11 in. across and sunk $\frac{1}{2}$ in. The peak was also of black leather. At each side were 2 bands of leather in a 'V' shape which strengthened the shako, the 'V' terminating behind brass lion-heads which were the attachments for the chinstrap. The illustration shows a private of the Battalion or Centre Company with a red-and-white ball tuft. The Grenadier Company had a white ball and the Light Company a green ball. The helmet plate was of brass, round, and edged with oak and laurel leaves and ribbons surmounted by a crown. In the centre, on a background of horizontal lines, the number 24 was in raised numbers.

Uniform

The coatee was of red cloth, the front being ornamented with white worsted tape button loops, with a button on each tape. The collar was of green cloth edged in white tape with a central taped line. The cuffs were of green cloth with a slashed flap ornamented in white tape with 4 buttons. The tails had false turnbacks in white, being joined at the bottom of the tail by a regimental-pattern button. The tails were decorated by a slashed flap with white tape and 4 regimental-pattern buttons. Above the slashed flaps at the waist were 2 buttons. Epaulettes were of green cloth edged in white tape and fringed with white cord, held in place by a regimental-pattern button. The button was of brass with a scalloped edge with the number 24 within a wreath. The trousers were of white cloth.

Accoutrements

Two buff crossbelts were worn, 1 over the left shoulder and 1 over the right, held together on the front by a crossfelt plate. The crossbelt passing over the left shoulder held a large black pouch for ammunition, and the 1 over the right shoulder had a frog for the bayonet.

The pack was made of canvas, reinforced with leather, and was worn by means of leather straps going round each arm. On top of the pack was a blanket held on by straps and the canteen was strapped on the back of the pack.

Weapons. Musket (Plate 96 B), Bayonet (Plate 96 B).

NOTE. In the background are a drummer and bandsman of the regiment.

70. 92nd Foot. Private, 1840

Head Dress

The bonnet was of black ostrich feathers 12 in. high. The headband was of diced cloth, the colours being red, white and green. Six ostrich-feather tassels hung down on the right side. A black cloth rosette was worn on the left side with the regimental device in the centre. A white plume was worn on the left side, coming from behind the rosette.

Uniform

The tailed coat was of red cloth, the front being taped and buttoned in pairs. The collar was of yellow cloth edged all round in white tape and decorated with a button loop at each end. The cuffs were of yellow cloth ornamented with a red slashed panel with buttons and button loops. The epaulettes were of yellow cloth edged in white tapes and ending in worsted tufts. The tails were turned back and lined in white cloth, the tails decorated with slashed flaps with buttons and button loops. Two buttons each side of the centre vent were worn at the waist. The kilt was of regimental pattern in Gordon tartan. The hose were of red-and-white diced wool with white spats. A sporran on a white buff belt was worn.

Accoutrements

Two white buff leather crossbelts were worn joined on the chest by a regimental-pattern crossbelt plate. The belt over the left shoulder was attached to a black ammunition pouch. The belt over the right shoulder ended in a bayonet frog. A canvas and leather pack was worn on the back, held on with 2 buff straps going round each arm. On top of the pack was a blanket roll, and a canteen was strapped on the back of the pack.

Weapons. Musket and bayonet (Plate 96 B).

71. Madras Rifles. Officer, 1840

Head Dress

The undress head dress was a peaked cap in dark green cloth with a very broad top and a black embroidered button in the centre. The peak was of black leather, edged in silver lace. The headband of the cap was decorated with a wide piece of silver lace of regimental pattern. A silver badge was worn on the front. The chinstrap was of black patent leather.

Uniform

A short stable jacket of dark green cloth was worn in undress, fastening down the front by hooks and eyes. There were 2 stripes of silver lace about $1\frac{1}{2}$ in. wide, down both edges of the fastenings. The collar was of black cloth, edged all round with silver lace. The cuffs were pointed, also in black cloth, and were 4 in. deep with silver-lace edging. The bottom edge of the jacket was bordered by 1-in. silver lace. The welts and back seams were piped in black. The trousers were of dark green cloth.

Accoutrements

A crimson sash was worn at the waist, with tassels hanging down the left side. A black waist-belt was worn over the sash, fastening in front with a snake fastening. Two sword slings were attached, hanging down the left side.

Weapon. Sword (Plate 91 I). In the Rifles the hilt was silver with bugle horn in lieu of Royal cipher.

72. 30th Madras Native Infantry. Officer, 1840

Head Dress

The shako was made of black beaver 6¾ in. high, the top covered in glazed leather and measuring 11 in. across. The top was sunk in ½ in. The sides were strengthened with a 'V' formation of leather. The chin scales were of overlapping gilt brass scales, backed with velvet. The shako plate was a large star plate surmounted by a crown, with a design according to regimental pattern.

Uniform

The coatee was of scarlet cloth, double-breasted with 2 rows of buttons down the front, 10 buttons in each row, set in pairs. The collar was of yellow cloth, decorated with 2 button loops in gold lace and regimental buttons on each end. The epaulettes were of gold lace, the shoulder board measuring 5 in. long and ending in a crescent, and gold-bullion fringes. The cuffs were of yellow cloth, decorated with a slashed flap with button loops in gold lace, each loop ornamented with a button in the centre. The tails were turned back and lined in white, the base of the tails decorated with a regimental device. The tails were decorated with a slashed pocket flap, the loops being in gold lace and ornamented with 4 buttons, 1 on each loop. Two buttons were worn at the back waist, just below the crimson sash. The trousers were of blue cloth with a red stripe running down the outside seam.

Accoutrements

A white buff crossbelt was worn, done up on the centre with a cross-belt plate of regimental pattern. The belt hung down on the left side, ending in a sword frog.

Weapon. Seword (Plate 91 I). In the East India Company Army the Royal cipher on the hilt was replaced by the company's crest.

73. Ceylon Regiment. Naik, 1840

Head Dress

The head dress was made of cane, covered in black cloth, the shape being reminiscent of the Guards' bearskin. Diagonally across the front was a dark green pugaree terminating in a dark green rosette on the top right-hand side. On the top was a large green tulip-shaped ornament. The close-up shows the pattern of shako worn by the officers.

Uniform

The coat was of dark green cloth with black collar and cuffs. The collar was edged in dark green tape. The cuffs had a green slashed flap ornamented with regimental buttons. The coat was double-breasted, having two rows of regimental-pattern buttons down the front, 7 buttons in each row. The last button in each row was worn under the red-and-black striped barrel sash. The short skirts had false turnbacks with a regimental button at the bottom. The skirts were decorated with slashed flaps with 4 buttons on each flap. Two buttons were worn at the back below the barrel sash. The epaulettes had black boards 5 in. long terminating in a black fringe. The trousers were of dark green cloth. No boots or shoes were worn, although some type of sandal might have been worn.

Accoutrements

A white buff leather crossbelt was worn over the left shoulder, fixing on to a black leather ammunition pouch. The bayonet was worn slung on the left side by means of a waist-worn belt under the barrel sash.

Weapons. Rifle, Sword bayonet (Plate 94 B).

74. Honourable East India Company College, Addiscombe. Cadet, 1844

Head Dress

The bell-top shako was made of black beaver $6\frac{3}{4}$ in. high. The top was covered in leather and measured 11 in. across. The top was sunk in $\frac{1}{2}$ in. The sides were strengthened with 2 pieces of leather in a 'V' formation. The chinchain on this particular pattern could be worn hooked up on the right side or in the usual manner. The chinchain fixed on to the helmet by means of brass lionheads. The plume holder was of brass with a white hair plume fitted. The helmet plate is thought to have been a brass star plate, surmounted by a crown with, in the centre, the arms of the Honourable East India Company with a gun beneath.

Uniform

The coatee was of blue cloth with red collar and cuffs. The collar was 3 in. high and decorated with twisted cords and 1 button on each side. The cuffs were 3 in. high and decorated with 3 buttons. The epaulettes were of gold lace, the boards being 5 in. long and ending in a crescent and gold-lace fringe. The boards were decorated with the arms of the East India Company. The coatee was single-breasted, with 10 buttons down the front, the last button worn underneath the waist-belt. The tails of the coatee were turned back and lined in red. They were decorated with slashed flap pockets ornamented with 3 buttons. Two buttons were worn at the back below the waist-belt. The trousers were of blue cloth with a red stripe down the outside seam.

Accoutrements

The waist-belt was of black leather, fastening in the front with a rectangular gilt plate bearing the arms of the Honourable East India Company.

Weapons. None.

NOTE. In the background is a Cadet in the undress uniform of the College. The close-up shows the crest of the Honourable East India Company.

75. 60th Rifles. Officer, 1845

Head Dress

A brown fur busby, about 10 in. high, was worn with no decoration at all.

Uniform

A large overcoat of dark green cloth, and brown fur, was worn. The collar was of brown fur. The coat was single-breasted with 5 olivets down the front as fastenings. Each olivet was decorated with black cord button loops. From the waist down, the leading edge was bordered in brown fur, as was the bottom edge of the coat. Large brown fur gloves were also worn. Canada boots were worn, which were large black leather leggings.

Accoutrements

A black leather crossbelt and pouch was worn. The crossbelt was ornamented with a silver lionhead, chain and whistle, and the regimental badge, also in silver. The black flap pouch was decorated with a stringed bugle horn, within the strings and the number 60, the whole surmounted by a crown. The waist-belt was of black leather, fastening in front with a snake buckle, 2 sword slings hanging down on the left side.

Weapon. Sword (Plate 91 I). In the 60th the hilt was silver with a bugle horn in lieu of Royal cipher.

Historical Note. The uniform described was worn by the 60th Rifles as winter dress in Canada.

76. Hyderabad Artillery. Officer, 1845

Head Dress

The turban was of blue cloth, edged around the headband in gold lace with a gold-lace button on the front. A line of gold lace ran diagonally right to left across the turban, with tassels hanging down on the top right-hand side. A yellow cloth decoration was worn on top.

Uniform

The coatee was of blue cloth, single-breasted, with 14 buttons down the front. One button out of 2 was ornamented with open bastion-ended lace. The last button was hidden by the crimson waist-sash. The collar was of red cloth, laced all round, and decorated with a gold-lace tab. The cuffs were also of red cloth and decorated with 3 regimental-pattern buttons and button loops. The tails were turned back, lined in red cloth and decorated with pocket flaps. Two buttons were worn at the waist, just below the crimson waist-sash. The epaulettes were of red cloth, edged in gold lace and ending in a gold-bullion fringe. The trousers were of grey cloth with a red stripe down the outside seam.

Accoutrements

A white buff leather crossbelt was worn over the right shoulder, with 2 sword slings hanging on the left side. The crossbelt was held together on the chest by a crossbelt plate of regimental pattern.

Weapon. Sword (Plate 91 I). The cartouche or oval in the hilt possibly bore the arms of Hyderabad.

77. 65th Bengal Native Infantry.
Sepoy, Light Company, 1845

Head Dress

The shako was made of black felt, the top being slightly wider than the base, which gave a slightly belled shape. The top was decorated with a piece of yellow worsted tape, as was the headband. A brass plume holder with a green worsted ball tuft was worn on top. The chain scales were of brass overlapping scales backed in leather. The shako plate was a small brass star of regimental pattern.

Uniform

The coatee was of red cloth, single-breasted, the front being buttoned in pairs, each button decorated with a white tape button loop. The collar was of yellow cloth, edged all round with white tape. The epaulettes were of red cloth, edged all round in white tape, the wing ends were also of red cloth, decorated in white tape and ended in white worsted tufts. The cuffs were of yellow cloth ornamented with 4 button loops in white tape. The tapes had a regimental button

at the top. The skirts were turned back, lined in white and decorated with pocket flaps. The trousers were of white cloth.

Accoutrements

Two buff crossbelts were worn, joined together on the chest by a crossbelt plate of regimental pattern. The belt over the left shoulder carried the large ammunition pouch. The 1 on the right shoulder ended on the left hip in a bayonet frog. A black canvas and leather pack was worn by means of 2 shoulder-straps, worn over the shoulder and then fixing back on to the pack.

Weapons. Musket and bayonet (Plate 93 E).

78. Royal Artillery. Officer, 1846

Head Dress

From this date until 1855 the Royal Artillery wore what was called the Albert shako. It was $6\frac{3}{4}$ in. high and $6\frac{1}{4}$ in. in diameter at the top. The body of the shako was of black beaver with a lacquered black leather top, and a lacquered thin black band around the bottom with a false buckle at the rear. The chinchain was tapered from wide at the rosette fitments on each side to narrow under the chin, and they were richly embossed and backed with leather and dark blue-black velvet. Both the front peak and the smaller back peak were of lacquered black leather. The plume was all white cut feathers with a gilt ring to prevent its splaying out, and it was held in a large gilt grenade plume holder with the Royal cipher on it. The gilt grenade hid the plume socket. The shako plate was a large 8-pointed star in gilt, on which was pinned the design of the Royal arms with supporters, and below which was a scroll with the motto *Ubique*. Below this was a gun facing left with another scroll underneath and the further motto *Quo fas et Gloria Ducunt*. The other ranks' pattern was similar but die-struck.

Uniform

The coatee was dark blue double-breasted with 10 buttons of regimental pattern. These buttons were of gilt, with a scalloped edge with a crown surmounting 3 guns, placed horizontally below. The collar and cuffs were scarlet, the collar being 3 in. high. On each side of the collar were gold-embroidered grenades. The rest of the collar was richly decorated in oak-leaf embroidery. The cuffs were plain scarlet with a slashed panel on each sleeve, and 3 regimental-pattern buttons, the whole slashed panel richly embroidered in oak-leaf design. The turnbacks were scarlet, as was the lining, and they had an embroidered ornament at the join at the bottom of the skirt. There were 2 buttons at the waist at the back, both sides of the centre vent. The epaulettes were of gold lace with bullion crescents and fringes and had a silver grenade embroidered on each. These were held by a small regimental button. A crimson sash was worn around the waist, knotting on the left side,

hanging down and ending in knots and tassels. The trousers were of blue cloth the same as the coatee, with a broad scarlet stripe 1¾ in. down the outer side seam.

Accoutrements

A white buff crossbelt was worn over the right shoulder, terminating in 2 rings joined by a short connecting strap on the left hip and worn underneath the sash. On each ring were fitted a sling for the sword, the front 1 short and the rear 1 long. The crossbelt plate joined the belt on the chest and was a rectangular frosted plate with plain edge with the design of the Royal arms without supporters, below which was the motto *Ubique*. Below the scroll was a gun facing left with a further scroll beneath, with the words *Quo fas et Gloria Ducunt*.

Weapon. Sword (Plate 91 I).

NOTE. In the background is a gunner of the Foot Artillery wearing a similar uniform to that of the officer, but carrying a musket and wearing infantry pattern equipment.

79. 68th Foot. Sergeant, 1846

Head Dress

The Albert shako was adopted by the British Army in December 1843, and brought into general use in 1844. It was made of black felt, 6¾ in. high. The top was covered in lacquered leather and measured 6¼ in. across. There were 2 peaks, 1 in front and 1 behind, the latter being much smaller.

The chinchain was of interlocking rings backed with leather and attached to the helmet with rosettes. The helmet plate was round, edged in laurel and oak leaves and ribboned at the quarters, the whole surmounted by a crown. In the centre of the plate was the number 68 on a horizontally lined background. The plate was die-stamped in brass. The pom-pom was green.

Uniform

The coatee was of red cloth, double-breasted, with 10 buttons in each row, the last 1 in each row being hidden by the crimson waist-sash, from which tassels hung on the left side. The collar was of green cloth, taped all round with white tape, top and bottom, with a short white tape on both sides in the centre. The cuffs were of green cloth with a slashed panel on each ornamented with button loops and buttons. Each slashed panel was decorated with 4 regimental-pattern buttons. The epaulettes were of red cloth, ornamented with white tape. Being the wing-type epaulette, they were tufted at the shoulder. The tails of the coat had false turnbacks lined with white and decorated at the join by a button. The back of the coatee was decorated with a slashed panel in white tape decorated with 4 buttons. There were also 2 buttons at the waist behind, just below the crimson sash. The button was of white metal decorated with a stringed bugle horn and crown above, with the number 68 in the centre. The trousers were of white cloth.

Accoutrements

Two white buff leather crossbelts were worn, 1 over the left shoulder and 1 over the right, held together on the front by a square belt plate. A black ammunition pouch was attached to the belt passing over the left shoulder. The belt passing over the right shoulder had a frog for the bayonet. The belt plate shown in close-up was the pattern worn by officers. It was a gilt plate with the stringed bugle horn and crown in the centre, and the number 68 within the strings, surrounded by laurel leaves all in silver. Above and below this are the battle honours SALAMANCA, PYRENEES, NIVELLE, ORTHES and PENINSULA.

Weapons. Musket, Bayonet (Plate 96 D).

NOTE. The figure shown in the background is an officer of the same period.

80. 92nd Foot. Officer, 1846

Head Dress

The bonnet was made of black ostrich feathers, 14 in. in height. The headband was diced in red and white with a centre square of green. Six black ostrich-feather plumes hung down on the right-hand side. A black rosette was on the left side with a regimental badge in the centre. A white vulture-feather plume, 8 in. high, emerged from the back of the rosette.

Uniform

The coatee was of scarlet cloth, double-breasted with 2 rows of regimental buttons, 10 buttons in each row. The Prussian collar was of yellow cloth 3 in. deep with 2 gold-lace loops and small buttons at each end. The cuffs were plain round cuffs in yellow, $2\frac{3}{4}$ in. deep, with a slashed flap with 4 laced loops and buttons for decoration. The coatee skirts were turned back and lined in white kerseymere cloth, which was laced at the edges, and decorated with slashed flaps, each with 4 laced loops and buttons. The join at the bottom of the skirts was decorated with a device of regimental pattern. There was a gold-lace triangle at the waist between the 2 back buttons. The regimental lace was gold, but, unlike other regiments, had a black train running through it. The epaulettes were of gold lace, the strap being 5 in. long, decorated with a thistle and ending in a double crescent and bullion fringe. The kilt was of regimental pattern in Gordon tartan. The hose were of red-and-white dicing with white tops. The shoes were flat-heeled with a silver buckle on the instep. A plaid was worn in Gordon tartan.

Accoutrements

A white buff baldrick was worn over the right shoulder with a frog on the end to carry the broadsword. It fastened in the centre with a regimental-pattern crossbelt plate, as shown in close-up. A red silk sash was worn over the left shoulder, with 2 tassels hanging down on the right hip.

The dirk belt was of black leather, fastening in front with a snake buckle, the dirk hanging down on the right front. The sporran was of white goat hair; on the top was a silver mount with the regimental number and honours. The goat hair was decorated with 6 gold cords and tassels. The button shown was that worn by other ranks at the time.

Weapons. Broadsword and Dirk (Appendix, 2, F).

81. Madras Native Infantry. Band Sergeant, 1846

Head Dress

The shako worn by the band differed from that worn by the sepoys of the Madras Native Infantry. The sepoys' shako was bell-shaped but without a peak. The band and Band Sergeant wore a red cloth shako, slightly bell-shaped. The top was edged in a 2-in. band of gold lace with a cockade at the front. Behind the cockade was a plume holder in which was fitted a feather plume rising and falling as shown. A 1-in. band of lace encircled the shako at the bottom. The chin scales were of brass, fitted each side with a round boss, and tapering to tie under the chin. Gold caplines encircled the cap and hung down on to the black lacquered peak at the front. The lines fell from the back of the shako and fitted on to a hook at the left breast of the coatee.

Uniform

A white coatee was worn with red collar, cuffs, lapels and turnbacks.

The collar was edged in gold lace and was 3 in. high. The false lapels were red and buttoned back to form a plastron. The coatee fastened by hooks and eyes down the front. There were 14 rows of gold lace loops and buttons on the red lapels, set in pairs. A waist-sash was worn, knotted on the left side. The cuffs were red and round, with a slashed panel with gold-lace button loops. The epaulettes were gold straps with crescents and bullion fringes. The skirts had red turnbacks and were held with a regimental device. They had 2 slashed panels with gold lace and buttons each side. There were 2 buttons above the centre vent above the pleats. Three chevrons in gold indicated the rank. The trousers were blue with a red welt on the outer seam.

Accoutrements

A black leather belt was worn over the sash with a rectangular buckle. A frog was fitted to the belt on the left side to hold the sword.

Weapon. Sword (Plate 92 D & E).

NOTE. The close-up shows a sepoy's shako of the period.

82. Malta Fencible Regiment. Private, 1847

Head Dress

The Albert shako was authorised for use in the British Army on 4 December 1843. The body was of black felt 6¾ in. high, the top covered in leather 6¼ in. across. Two peaks were worn, 1 at the back and 1 at the front. The chinstrap was of leather fixed on to the shako by brass rosettes. The worsted tuft was green. The badge was a circle of laurel and oak leaves with ribbons at the quarters, the whole being surmounted by a crown. The centre was possibly the Cross of Malta with the words 'Malta Fencibles' underneath.

Uniform

The coatee was of red cloth with blue collar and cuffs. The collar was edged all round with white tape. There was also a central strand of tape on both sides of the collar, about 2 in. long. The blue cloth cuffs were approximately 3 in. deep, decorated with a slashed panel with 4 buttons of regimental pattern. The epaulettes were of blue cloth, decorated with white tape and ending in white worsted tufts. The coatee was single-breasted with 8 buttons down the front. The buttons were set in pairs and ornamented with white worsted button loops. The skirts were turned back and had pocket flaps, with 2 buttons at the waist. The trousers were of dark blue cloth with a red stripe down the outside seam.

Accoutrements

Two white buff leather crossbelts were worn, 1 over each shoulder. The 1 over the right shoulder carried the frog for the bayonet and the 1 over the left shoulder carried the ammunition pouch. The crossbelts were held together on the chest by a belt plate of regimental pattern. A large black canvas and leather pack was carried on the back with a bed-roll strapped above. This was worn with a strap passing over each shoulder and a joining strap going across the chest.

Weapons. Musket, Bayonet (Plate 96 D).

NOTE. The close-up shows an Albert shako with white tropical cover.

83. Honourable Artillery Company, Infantry. Officer, 1848

Head Dress

The head dress was the Albert shako authorised on 4 December 1843 and introduced generally in 1844. The body was of black beaver, $6\frac{3}{4}$ in. high, with a black lacquered leather top, $6\frac{1}{4}$ in. in diameter. Around the top and bottom of the shako was a band of black lacquered leather. There were 2 peaks of black lacquered leather, 1 at the front and another, much smaller one and more sloping, at the rear. The chinchain was of stamped brass interlocking rings fitted at each side of the shako under large gilt rosettes. The chinchain was wide at the sides and tapered to narrow under the chin. A white ball tuft was worn in a plume holder on the top front of the shako. The plate was a stamped silver star with a gilt grenade in the centre.

Uniform

The uniform was very similar to that worn by officers of the 1st Foot Guards. William IV had, in fact, granted permission to wear the same dress as the 1st or Grenadier Guards,

with silver lace instead of gold. The collar was 3 in. deep, of blue cloth, and closed at the front. The collar was decorated both sides with a panel of silver embroidery on to which was fitted a grenade in gold embroidery. The coat was double-breasted, the buttons spaced singly, as the Grenadier Guards. The cuffs were blue with a slashed panel ornamented with silver-lace loops and buttons. The skirts were lined in white, as were the turnbacks held back by an embroidered grenade. On each side of the skirts was a slashed panel of silver embroidery with buttons. A crimson sash was worn around the waist. White trousers were worn in summer dress. The epaulettes were silver with a gold grenade.

Accoutrements

A white buff crossbelt was worn over the right shoulder and terminated in a frog on the left hip. The belt was fastened on the chest with a large rectangular belt plate.

Weapon. Sword (Appendix 2, G).

Historical Note. The bearskin cap worn by the Grenadier Guards was not authorised for the Honourable Artillery Company until 1853.

NOTE. In the background is an officer in frock coat and forage cap.

84. Royal Dockyard Battalion. Private, 1848

Head Dress

The shako was made of black felt and measured about $6\frac{3}{4}$ in. high in the front and back. The top was of black leather sunk in $\frac{1}{2}$ in. At the top of the shako was a $1\frac{1}{2}$-in. band of yellow tape. The chinchain was of brass interlocking rings which fitted to the shako by lionhead bosses. There was also a hook on the back so that the chinchain could be worn hooked up, as shown in the illustration. The shako plate was of brass, oval in shape, the edge decorated with oak leaves. The whole was surmounted by a crown. In the centre was a large white-metal fouled anchor. At the bottom below the oak leaves were 3 scrolls bearing the title 'Royal Dockyard Battalion'. A red-and-white pom-pom was worn on the top.

Uniform

The frock coat was of blue cloth, double-breasted, with 2 rows of buttons down the front, 8 buttons in each row. The collar was of scarlet. The cuffs were pointed and decorated, with 1 button on the scarlet and 1 button on the blue. The epaulettes were of scarlet cloth, the boards being 5 in. in length, ending in a crescent. The skirts at the back were very plain with 2 regimental-pattern buttons at the top, worn below the waist-belt. The trousers were of blue cloth with a single scarlet stripe down the outside seam.

Accoutrements

A plain black leather waist-belt was worn, fastening in front by means of a rectangular brass plate, bearing the badge of the Dockyard Battalion. A black frog hung down on the left hip to carry the bayonet.

Weapons. Musket, Bayonet (Plate 96 D).

Historical Note. Officers of the Royal Dockyard Battalion wore the Royal Navy pattern sword with the words 'Royal Dockyard Battalion' on the blade.

85. Hyderabad Infantry. Officer, 1848

Head Dress

The turban was of blue cloth edged round the headband in gold lace with a red worm running through it. A line of gold lace with a red worm on each edge ran diagonally left to right across the turban, with tassels hanging on the top left side. A yellow cloth decoration was worn on top.

Uniform

The coatee was of scarlet cloth, single-breasted with 11 buttons down the front, the last button being hidden by the crimson waist-sash, which had tassels hanging down on the left side. The collar was of green cloth, edged all round in gold lace. The round cuffs were of green cloth and decorated with buttons and gold-lace button loops. The epaulettes were of green cloth edged in gold lace, the wing ends being in red cloth, decorated with a gold-bullion fringe. The skirts were turned back, lined in white and decorated with pocket flaps with buttons and gold-lace button loops. The trousers were of white cloth.

Accoutrements

A white buff leather crossbelt was worn over the right shoulder, fastening on the chest with a crossbelt plate of regimental pattern. This crossbelt had a sword frog hanging on the left hip.

Weapon. Sword (Plate 91 I). The cartouche or oval probably bore the arms of Hyderabad.

86. 57th Foot. Private, Grenadier Company, 1849

Head Dress

The head dress worn was authorised on 4 December 1843 and known as the Albert shako. It continued to be worn by infantry until on 16 January 1855 the second pattern Albert was authorised. It was of black felt, $6\frac{3}{4}$ in. high and $6\frac{1}{4}$ in. across. The top was of black lacquered leather, as was the peak at the front and the small sloping peak at the rear. A band of lacquered leather ran around the bottom of the shako with a false buckle at the rear. Other ranks wore a black leather chinstrap, whereas the warrant officers and officers wore chin scales. A rosette was worn on both sides of the shako on the bottom band. A ball tuft was worn at the top centre front, white for Grenadier company, green for Light company and white over red for Centre or Battalion company. The shako plate was of stamped brass, a circle surmounted by a crown. The circle had a raised border of oak leaves on the left and laurel and berries on the right, bound at the top and bottom, and both sides, with crossed bands of ribbon. In the centre, on a horizontally lined ground, was the number 57. The shako was known as the Albert because it was reputed to have been introduced at the suggestion of the Prince Consort.

Uniform

A red coatee was worn with 3-in.-high collar of regimental face colour, in this case yellow, with cuffs of the same colour. The coatee was single-breasted with 10 bands of white tape and 10 buttons, with the design 57 below the word 'Albuhera' within a laurel wreath, and with a crown above the word 'Albuhera'. The tape was plain white, regimental-pattern tape having been abolished on 10 October 1836 by Royal Warrant (except for Drummers). The cuffs were slashed with buttons and tape, the collar had a plain white tape on both front edges and was edged all round in white tape. The turnbacks were of white and buttoned with a regimental-pattern button. There were also 2 buttons at the waist. The back was completely plain, slashed flaps having been abolished in 1848. The epaulettes were of the wing pattern, of worsted tuft with a strap of the face colour, yellow, edged in white tape. These epaulettes were Flank company only, the Battalion company having tufts in lieu of the wing. Trousers were of a blue indigo mixture with a red welt on the outer seam of each leg.

Accoutrements

Two white buff crossbelts were worn, the 1 over the left shoulder suspended the large black leather ammunition pouch on the right hip and the 1 over the right shoulder held the bayonet in a frog on the left hip. The belt plate in the centre of the chest was in die-stamped brass with the raised design of a large crown above the numbers 57. Above the crown in a scroll and nearly stretching the width of the plate was the word ALBUHERA. Beneath the number 57 and flanking it on both sides were two branches of laurels and berries tied at the base with ribbon. (The officers' design was highly elaborate and decorative having a cut silver star of the Grand Cross of the Order of the Bath and enriched with enamels. Below was the number and the honours were inscribed on the rays of the cross. The belt suspending the ammunition box had a brass buckle slide and tip for adjustment. A large black canvas pack was worn, reinforced with leather at the corners and along the top. The sides were lined in wood and the pack opened at the back. In the centre the regimental number was painted. On the back a blanket or greatcoat was rolled. When worn, the 'D'-shaped mess tin was strapped to the top of the pack. The water-bottle worn in marching order was painted blue and was like a squat barrel with the letters B.O. (Board of Ordnance) and a broad arrow in the centre. It was worn on a strap over the right shoulder, the barrel resting on the white haversack worn also on a strap over the right shoulder.

Weapons. Musket, Bayonet (Plate 96 D).

NOTE. In the background is an officer in undress shell jacket and forage cap, and the back view of a private.

87. 7th Foot.
Sergeant Major, 1850

Head Dress

The Albert shako was sanctioned for the British Army on 4 December 1843. The body was of black felt, $6\frac{3}{4}$ in. high, with a black leather top $6\frac{1}{4}$ in. across. The top and bottom of the shako were bound in leather. Two peaks were fitted, 1 small one at the back and 1 at the front. The chinchain was of brass, and tapered, fixing on to the sides of the shako with brass rosettes. A white ball tuft was worn on the top of the shako. The shako plate for the 7th was a large brass grenade, the design on the bomb being a crowned Garter with the Tudor rose in the centre.

Uniform

The coatee was of scarlet cloth, double-breasted with 2 rows of buttons down the front, 10 buttons in each row, worn in pairs. The collar was of blue cloth ornamented by 2 buttons and silver-lace button loops at each end. The cuffs were of blue cloth, decorated with a slashed flap with silver-lace button loops, each loop having a button in the centre. The wing epaulettes were of linked silver chains edged all round in silver lace, the wing ending in silver fringe. The shoulder board was decorated with a brass grenade. The tails of the coatee were turned back and lined in white, the base of the tails decorated with a regimental device. Two regimental-pattern buttons were worn at the waist below the crimson waist-sash. The trousers were of dark blue cloth with a scarlet welt running down the outside seam. The crimson waist-sash was worn at the waist, with cords and tassels hooking up on to the second button on the right side of the coatee.

Accoutrements

A white buff leather crossbelt was worn over the right shoulder, ending in a sword frog hanging on the left side. The crossbelt was decorated with a crossbelt plate and slide. The crossbelt plate was in gilt brass and enamels.

Weapon. Sword (Plate 91 I).

NOTE. The close-up shows the belt plate described above.

88. 74th Foot. Officer, 1850

Head Dress

In 1845 the 74th Foot were again designated a Highland regiment, and changed many of their accoutrements to a Scottish style. The shako they wore at this period was of black beaver 6¾ in. in height, the top being 6¼ in. across and covered in leather. A black patent leather peak was worn on the front, but unlike other Line regiments, no back peak was worn. A black corded boss was worn on the top front of the shako, decorated with a gilt thistle. A red-and-white pom-pom was fitted into a plume holder hidden behind the boss. The badge on the front was similar in shape to the Order of the Thistle, but was decorated with regimental honours and titles. The headband of the shako was decorated with a white, red and green diced border. The shako was further decorated with black plaited silk cords which were attached to the sides of the shako, hung down in front and were hooked to the peak. The caplines were of black silk, attached to the right side of the cap, passed round the body once under the plaid and connected up high on the left side under the plaid. The chinchain was gilt brass linked chain, backed on to black velvet and held on each side with a round gilt boss.

Uniform

The coatee was of scarlet cloth, double-breasted with 2 rows of buttons, 10 in each row, according to regimental pattern. The collar was of white cloth, 3 in. high, and decorated with 2 gold-lace loops with a button at each end. The cuffs were 2¾ in. deep in white cloth, decorated with a slashed flap with 4 laced loops and buttons. The tails were turned back and lined in white, the bottom decorated with a regimental device. The epaulettes were of gold lace with shoulder boards 5 in. long, with a crescent and fringing at the end. The crescent was decorated with a thistle. The trews were of Lamont tartan, which was similar to the Black Watch tartan, except that it had a white over-stripe. The plaid was also of Lamont tartan and was worn around the chest, hanging down on the left side. It was fixed to the left shoulder by a plaid brooch. A red sash was worn under the plaid over the left shoulder, the tassels hanging on the right side.

Accoutrements

One white baldrick was worn over the right shoulder, fastening on the front by means of a crossbelt plate. The baldrick had a fitment for the sword, hanging on the left side. The belt plate was a gilt plate, with the Order of the Thistle in silver, mounted in the centre, decorated with the title '74th Highlanders' and the honours of the regiment. The waist-belt was of gold lace, fastened at the front by a gilt rectangular plate with the badge in the centre. The dirk was worn fitted on to slings on the front right side.

Weapons. Broadsword, Dirk (Appendix 2, F).

Historical Note. Memorandum from the War Office dated 8 November 1845: 'Her Majesty has been graciously pleased to approve of the 74th Foot resuming the appellation of the 74th (Highland) Regiment of Foot, and of its being clothed accordingly, that is, to wear the tartan trews instead of the Oxford mixture; plaid cap instead of black shako; and the plaid scarf as worn by the 71st Regiment. The alteration of the dress is to take place on the next issue of clothing, on 1st April, 1846.'

89. 88th Foot. Corporal, 1854

Head Dress

The head dress shown was the undress forage cap or, as it was called, the 'porkpie' hat. This name derived from its shape. It was made of blue cloth with a blue-black pom-pom on the top. The regimental distinction was by means of brass numerals on the front. The cap was worn in lieu of the Albert shako.

Uniform

A red coatee was worn, with the collar and cuffs of regimental face colour. The coatee was single-breasted with 8 rows of plain white tape and 8 buttons. The tapes were grouped in pairs. The cuffs were yellow with a slashed panel with 4 button loops and buttons. The collar was edged in white tape with a button loop both sides. The epaulettes had yellow straps edged in white tape and with a white worsted tuft on the shoulder. The turnbacks were white and joined with a regimental button. There were 2 buttons at the waist at the back. The trousers were blue with a red welt on the outer seam.

Accoutrements

The illustration shows the soldier wearing the improved equipment, introduced in 1850. The crossbelt with the regimental-pattern plate, which held the bayonet, had now been abolished, and the bayonet was carried in a frog from a waist-belt. The ammunition pouch was still carried on a crossbelt going over the left shoulder. The waist-belt held the bayonet on the left hip. The haversack was worn on the left side, the strap going over the right shoulder. The round water-bottle hung on the right hip, its belt passing over the left shoulder. A secondary ammunition pouch was worn on the belt at the right front when in action. A small buff pouch was fitted to the cross-belt, to carry the percussion caps for the rifle. A large black canvas pack was worn on the back and suspended by shoulder-straps and a connecting strap across the chest. A blanket was rolled on top of this, and a mess-tin in an oil-skin cover carried, strapped to the top of the pack.

Weapons. Enfield rifle (Plate 96 A), Bayonet (Plate 96 A).

NOTE. The close-up shows the officer's shako plate, 1844–55.

90. 41st Bengal Native Infantry. Sepoy, 1855

Head Dress

The pillbox hat worn was of black felt. It was about $2\frac{1}{2}$ in. high and $6\frac{1}{2}$ in. across the top. Brass numerals were worn at the front. The illustration shows the white cover being worn, which buttoned up on the left side. The number on the front denoted the regiment.

Uniform

The coat was of red cloth, single-breasted with 8 buttons in pairs down the front, each pair having 2 button loops in white tape. The collar was of yellow cloth, edged all round with white tape. The yellow epaulettes were edged all round with white tape and ended in a white worsted fringe. The cuffs were of yellow cloth, decorated with 4 buttons and button loops in pairs. The skirts were turned back and lined in white. The skirts were decorated with flap pockets with buttons and tapes. Two buttons were worn at the waist on the back, below the waist-belt. The trousers were of white cloth.

Accoutrements

Two crossbelts were worn, joined together on the chest by a regimental-pattern crossbelt plate. The belt over the left shoulder carried the ammunition box, and the belt over the right shoulder carried the bayonet. A black canvas and leather pack was worn on the back, fastening with a strap going under both arms, and a strap joining the 2 going across the chest.

Weapons. Musket and bayonet (Plate 93 E).

APPENDIX 1

Plate 91

A. *1803 Pattern.* General Orders dated 18 March 1803 introduced this sword for general officers and officers of Infantry of the Line. In the case of general officers, the grip was in ivory, carved with grooves, into which was bound a triple strand of gold or gilt wire. All other officers who carried the sword had a grip of wood, covered with blackened fishskin and then similarly bound with gilt wire. The front of the guard bore the cipher of King George III, surmounted by a crown. Flank company officers' swords bore also, above the crown, the insignia of their particular company: a grenade for Grenadier companies and a bugle horn, stringed, for Light companies.

In all cases the sword was carried in a black leather scabbard with 3 gilt mounts, the middle mount bearing a ring for sling suspension and the top mount bearing both a ring and a stud, which made it possible for the sword to be carried, either in a frog or from a belt and slings. The sealed pattern of this sword in the Tower of London, is in a maroon velvet scabbard, but this was, it is thought, the Duke of York's own sword, as Commander-in-Chief.

B. *1831 Pattern for general officers.* The Duke of Wellington became Commander-in-Chief in 1827, and, in 1831, there was introduced a sword for general officers with a hilt in ivory in the pattern of that carried by the Mamelukes, who had, at the time, recently been exterminated in Egypt, by Mehemet Ali, after ruling for 600 years. The brass crossguard of this sword was heavily firegilt and bore in the centre of both sides the rank badge of a general.

The scabbard was in polished brass and terminated in a large rounded shoe. At a later date the shoe became smaller and square, and in 1898 the scabbard was ordered to be nickel-plated.

C. *1796 Pattern.* Although this sword was in regulation use, before this date by practically all dismounted officers, it was not until 1796 that General Orders prescribed it officially. The shell guard was, in some cases, hinged at its mid-point, so that it would fall flat against the body of the wearer, but others were fixed. The grip was bound with twisted wire, 2 strands with an alternative direction of twist being used, giving a herringbone effect. The blade was straight, single-edged and engraved with the Royal cipher and trophies of arms. On some swords this engraving was gold-filled, in which case the blade was invariably blued for at least half its length. The scabbard was black leather with 3 gilt mounts, the middle and top mounts having rings for sling suspension, and the top mount having also a stud for use in a frog.

Field officers carried the sword in a polished steel scabbard, suspended from slings.

D. *Grenadier Guards Senior N.C.O.* (*c.* 1816). Senior N.C.O.s of the Regiments of Foot Guards carried a prescribed regimental-pattern of sword which was similar in size, but distinctive in pattern. The hilt was, in all cases, polished brass and the grip either leather or fishskin bound with gilt wire. The blade was slightly curved and the weapon was carried in a black leather scabbard with top and bottom mounts. The top mount bore a stud for frog suspension.

E. *Scots Guards Senior N.C.O.* (*c.* 1803). See above.

F. *Infantry Officer* (*c.* 1780). In the days before regulation weapons officers carried the sword selected by their commanding officer. This particular pattern was that of the 35th Regiment of Foot. The hilt was in firegilt brass and the grip bound with twisted silver wire. The blade in this case was 2-edged, of flattened diamond section, and was carried in a black leather scabbard, with 2 brass mounts. It was worn suspended from a frog.

G. *Volunteer Infantry Officer* (*c.* 1800). The patterns of sword carried by Volunteers were many and varied, but this particular pattern was probably the most commonly adopted. The knucklebow, pommel and ferrule were in firegilt brass, and the grip was in black horn. It was bisected by a gilt band bearing a cartouche inscribed with the badge and name of the particular regiment. The scabbard was invariably in black leather and was usually mounted at only the top and bottom, and fitted for wear in a frog or baldrick.

H. *Infantry Officer's Pattern of 1786.* On 3 April 1786 King George III gave orders for a strong cut-and-thrust sword for officers of the Infantry of the Line, the hilt mounts to be in silver or gold-coloured metal, to match the buttons of the uniform. This sword was of similar design to the one described above. The knucklebow, however, was decorated with a cluster of 5 balls, and a similar decoration was placed on the small counter guard that lay on the outside of the cross guard. The grip, of ivory, was bisected by a metal band bearing the name and badge of the regiment. The scabbard was of black leather with 2 mounts, the top one equipped with a stud for frog suspension. This particular example was in sterling silver, but examples in plated base metal are more numerous.

I. *Infantry Officer, 1822 Pattern.* Dress Regulations for all Regiments of Foot described the 1822 pattern sword, as follows,

'Gilt half-basket with G IV R inserted in the outward bars and lined with black patent leather. Grip of black fishskin, bound with three gilt wires.

The blade $32\frac{1}{2}$ in. in length with round back terminating to a shampre within 9 in. of the point and a very little curved. Scabbard black with gilt mountings, steel in the field. To be carried by Garrison Staff, Royal Military Asylum, Provost Marshal, Medical, Commissariat, Paymaster, Judge Advocate, Foot Guards and Infantry of the Line.'

In 1831 the blade was narrowed to 1 in. at the hilt, and in 1834 all field officers were ordered to adopt a brass scabbard. The design of the blade caused much discussion, due to the ramrod back interfering with a good clean cut, and Henry Wilkinson is credited with the remark, 'The worst damn sword with which the British officer was ever equipped.' With a blade redesigned by Wilkinson in 1841, the sword remained in service until 1895.

Plate 92

A. The Royal Engineers were ordered, in 1856, to carry a sword with a slightly curved blade and with a hilt in gunmetal. This hilt, of scroll design, was the same as the cavalry officer in heavy regiments had been ordered in steel. Later, field officers of the Black Watch, H.L.I., Seaforth Highlanders and the Argyll & Sutherland Highlanders carried this hilt in nickel-plate as an alternative to the basket hilt on their broadswords.

B. In the mid-eighteenth century private soldiers carried a hanger with a hilt in polished brass and with a ball-shaped pommel. The grip was bound in brass wire. The blade was of medium length, about $27\frac{1}{2}$ in., and the sword was carried in a black leather scabbard with polished brass mounts, the top mount being fitted with a stud for carriage in a frog or baldrick.

C. In 1831 pioneers in infantry regiments were equipped with a fearsome weapon in place of the normal infantry hanger. This had a broad, slightly curved blade $26\frac{1}{2}$ in. in length, and the hilt was in polished brass with the grip and backpiece cast as one and, being a drive fit on to the tang of the blade, the knucklebow was stirrup-shaped in brass. The frightful feature of this weapon was the back of the blade, which incorporated a crosscut saw for 18 in. of its length and terminated in a double spear point for the last $7\frac{1}{2}$ in. Designed as both an axe and a saw for use in constructing field works, it was nevertheless their fighting weapon, and as such created frightful wounds.

D. and **E.** The first 2 weapons shown are more decorative than useful, and belong to the latter part of the eighteenth century and the first quarter of the nineteenth. They were specific to the regimental band, known in those days as the regimental music, and the designs varied with the particular regiment.

The two shown are, on the left, that of the 48th Northamptonshire Regiment, and, in the centre, that of a Scottish Line regiment.

F. Although pioneers carried the sword shown above, certain regiments had their own specific design of hilt. One of these regiments was the 52nd (Oxfordshire) Light Infantry Regiment, and this elaborate hilt, fitted to the standard blade, carried their regimental number and a stringed bugle horn in raised characters on the sides of the slab-sided grip.

G. The music of the infantry regiments were ordered a new sword in 1850. This weapon had a straight blade, varying between 21 and 24 in. in length, and the hilt, consisting of grip and crossguard, was cast in one piece of brass. The design of the grip was faintly Gothic, and the centre of the crossguard was a square cartouche which bore a raised casting of the Royal cipher or, in the case of Light Infantry, a bugle horn stringed. The particular weapon shown bears a grenade and was specific to the Grenadier Regiment of Foot Guards.

H. At the time of the Battle of Waterloo foot artillery privates carried a brass-hilted hanger with a slightly curved blade. The grip and knucklebow were cast in one piece of brass and the blade was about 23 in. long. It was carried in a black leather scabbard with 2 brass mounts, the top one bearing a stud for frog or baldrick suspension. This weapon design was common to a number of continental armies at the period, and was not specific to artillery in these armies.

I. At the time of the Crimean war the old Corps of Royal Waggoners, who had been disbanded in 1833, were raised again as the Land Transport Corps, and the private soldiers were equipped with a cross-hilted hanger of a design borrowed from either the French or the Prussian Armies, both of whom had carried it for some years. The hilt, cast in one piece of brass, was a drive fit on to the tang of the blade, which was straight, double-edged and about 19 in. long. Some blades can be found that are in the shape of a sage leaf, and are copied from the old Roman short sword design. Carried in a frog or baldrick, the black leather scabbard had 2 brass mounts with a stud on the top one.

LONG ARMS

Plate 93

The Land pattern muskets in this plate span the years from 1730 to 1760. Land pattern in this context is a nomenclature to designate the use by soldiers as opposed to Navy and Marines. As can be seen from the plate, these weapons all employed the use of flint and steel to generate a spark that would ignite a primary charge of gunpowder in a pan connected by a small channel to the barrel of the musket where the main charge had been placed. The placing of this main charge was through the barrel, hence the general description of flintlock muzzle loaders.

The popular name of 'Brown Bess' which was used for these weapons has its origin surrounded in mystery, and no authority has yet been able to suggest a plausible reason for the adoption of such a soubriquet.

A. The long Land pattern musket of c. 1731, in use from approximately 1715 until superseded by a new sealed pattern in about 1745. Characterised by the 46-in. barrel and the long fore end.

B. The sealed pattern long Land musket of c. 1745. Also with a 46-in. barrel of 17 or musket bore, but with a slightly shorter fore end.

C. The short Land musket known as the new Militia pattern. This was specifically designed to meet the demand for a musket to arm the increasing number of recruits for the Militia, in the late 1750s. Its main characteristic was the use of a 42-in. barrel. It was also adopted for use by Marines, who had found the previous 46-in. model to be difficult to carry and store between the decks of wooden-walled naval ships.

D. The light infantry carbine was introduced for those troops where the emphasis was on mobility. Although much care went into the design of carbines for Light Dragoons, Artillery and certain officers, the example shown in this plate was simply a lightened version of the short Land musket with the 42-in. barrel.

E. In 1780, under the threat of the Napoleonic wars, and ever-mindful of the cost of arming the increasingly large number of infantry that were being recruited to the colours, the Board of Ordnance introduced a cheaper version of the Land musket that had sufficed for the British Army since 1730. This became known as the India pattern, and was distinguished from its predecessors by its rather inferior finish and unpleasantly rough woodwork.

Plate 94

A. Introduced into the service by the Duke of Brunswick, this rifle had a 39-in. barrel, bored with 2 wide grooves of rifling which made a complete turn from muzzle to barrel plug. The ignition of the charge, which was muzzle-loaded, was by means of the percussion system, which incorporated a fulminate-of-mercury-filled copper cap which fitted on to a nipple screwed into the barrel. A hammer, actuated by the trigger, crushed the cap against the nipple, which was bored to allow the resulting burst of flame to enter the barrel and ignite the main charge.

B. The Baker rifle, so named after its designer Ezekiel Baker (a noted gun-maker), was brought into the service at the latter end of 1800; the model shown is the musket-bore Baker rifle, having the standard length barrel of 30 in. with 7 grooves of rifling and a calibre of approximately 0˙70 in. At the muzzle end there is a bar on the side to take the sword bayonet, illustrated alongside.

C. The Foot Guards carried a variation of the Brunswick rifle, for issue to sergeants. This weapon had a 39-in. barrel, but instead of being equipped with a bar to take a sword bayonet, as in A above, it was equipped with a socket bayonet as had been standard for the 'Brown Bess' (Plate 93).

D. This is the original version of the Brunswick, which was introduced in 1837, and it incorporated a back-action lock instead of the later side-action (A above), and had a rather inferior method of fastening the sword bayonet on to the bar.

E. Some models of the Baker rifle (B above) were adapted to mount the socket bayonet rather than the sword bayonet. To do this, it was necessary to shorten the fore end, allowing a protrusion of the barrel, and to remove from it the bayonet bar, welding on in its place a stud for locking the socket into place. The reasons behind this can only have been economy, in that it allowed stocks of old bayonets to be used, in place of the more expensive brass-hilted variety which had been designed for the rifle originally. The actual rifle was not otherwise altered, although it was claimed that its accuracy with bayonet fixed was superior with the socket bayonet, due to its lighter weight.

Plate 95

A. With the later models of Baker rifle, improvements that were suggested by the actual users were gradually incorporated. This particular illustration shows a model of about 1825, which had, incorporated in the lock, a safety bar, with which the hammer could be locked at full cock without any danger of the rifle being discharged accidentally. Also, the sides of the pan which held the priming charge were raised so that there was less chance of spillage when loading the weapon, and it gave more protection in damp weather, one of the main problems that the rifleman had to contend with. The bayonet had also come in for a lot of criticism, and the sword bayonet having finally been adjudged to be too heavy, a light model was introduced (cf. Plate 94 B).

B. In 1841 there was introduced a special carbine for Sappers & Miners. This weapon had a 30-in. barrel and was fired by the percussion system. The main distinctive feature of the original model was its unwieldy and costly bayonet, which incorporated a 3-bar guard, as in the cavalry sword, in addition to the socket by which it was attached to the muzzle. The blade was long and straight and incorporated a saw back. This bayonet lasted only a few years, and the model illustrated has the second pattern bayonet with a simple socket grip and without the saw back to the blade.

C. This illustration shows the last of the flintlock smooth-bore muskets in service with the British Army, and is probably the only flintlock weapon that was used during the reign of Queen Victoria. It was the final version of the India pattern (cf. Plate 93 E).

D. One of the series of new land arms was the sergeants' carbine, introduced in 1807. It was, in reality, only a smaller edition of the India-pattern musket (cf. Plate 93 E), and it had a 37-in. barrel of 0·65 in. bore, as opposed to musket bore, which was 0·75 in.

Plate 96

A. As a direct result of a competition between gunmakers, sponsored by the Board of Ordnance, a new rifle, known as the Pattern 1853 or Enfield, was introduced. This was a percussion weapon with a 39-in. barrel of 0·577 in., bore and rifled. The barrel was not pinned to the wooden fore end, as had been previous practice, but was attached by 3 steel bands. The weapon was sighted to fire up to 800 yards, an indication of the changing nature of warfare. For the bayonet, a return was made to the socket method of attachment.

B. In 1839 the last remaining India-pattern muskets (cf. Plate 95 C) were converted in limited numbers from flintlock to percussion. This conversion was purely in the method of firing the charge, and in all other respects the weapon remained a smooth-bore musket.

C. In 1851 the Duke of Wellington agreed to the Ordnance recommendation for the issue, to the infantry, of the French-designed Minie rifle. This weapon had but a short life with the British Army before being superseded by the pattern '53 Enfield (cf. A above). The barrel was 39 in. long and of 0·702 in. bore. However, the main feature of the weapon was the design of the bullet, which was the first practical attempt to get away from the round ball, resulting in a projectile which, by being elongated, increased greatly the weight of it for a comparable calibre, being about 40 per cent heavier than the old musket ball.

D. The pattern '42 percussion smooth-bore musket followed on the conversion of the old India-pattern muskets (cf. B above) and differed very little from them. Its introduction was agreed upon because of a disastrous fire that had occurred at the Tower of London in the latter part of 1841, and which had destroyed the Army's reserve of 280,000 firearms.

E. The Lancaster rifle was ordered in 1855 for the Royal Sappers & Miners and, except for its special feature of an oval bore and the sword bayonet with which it was equipped, its appearance was that of a shortened version of the pattern 1853 Enfield (cf. A above). It had a 32-in. barrel, and the average of the bore was 0·577 in., although the dimensions varied at both the muzzle and the breech, in both axes of the ovoid shape. The blade of the sword bayonet was of what is known as falchion shape and was 2 ft in length.

APPENDIX 2

A. 'Hanger', Infantry privates, *c.* 1751. This was akin to the weapon already described (plate 92b) but the guard was rather more involved, having several bars instead of the single knuckle bow. The Tower of London stores contain a great variety of these weapons, and it is safe to say that regimental patterns were purchased by Commanding Officers and they were not a government issue.

B. Highland Broadsword, *c.* 1750. This was the traditional weapon of the Scottish Highland Infantry and was a weapon with a two-edged cut-and-thrust blade. The variety of the enclosed basket hilt is such that one might find hundreds of examples of which no two are alike.

C. Spontoon, *c.* 1750. This was a staff weapon which was carried by officers and sergeants of Infantry regiments, on and off for nearly a hundred years. The head was at various times flamboyant and highly decorated and at others a simple pike and completely plain.

D. The Short Axe or Tomahawk. These were issued to both engineers and infantry pioneers, and the head was broad-bladed on one side and sharply pointed on the other. It was mounted on a short stout handle and was carried in a leather 'holster' on the belt.

E. Billhook. Pioneers and mounted officers' grooms carried a billhook. This was a straightforward horticultural implement, and for the pioneer it was used for cutting brushwood and clearing fields of fire, and for the groom it was a necessary implement for gathering fodder.

F. Highland Officers' Broadsword and Dirk. These companion weapons were the arms of Highland officers from the mid-eighteenth century onwards. The sword, known erroneously as a claymore, was a basket-hilted weapon with a two-edged thrusting blade. The hilt was normally of regimental pattern. The Dirk was a broad-bladed knife of some 15–18 in. overall, and the grip was a thistle carved in ebony. On the scabbard were minor scabbards for the carriage on a companion set of a knife and fork. Once again, the style was regimental.

G. In the second quarter of the nineteenth century officers of the Infantry battalions of the Honourable Artillery Company adopted, for wear with dress uniforms, a sword that was unlike any other regulation sword of the time and was akin to the swords carried by Volunteer officers at the turn of the century.

The knuckle-bow was of gilt brass and was stirrup shaped, decorated at the centre point with rosettes. The pommel was gilt brass and continued for about $1\frac{1}{2}$ in. down the grip which was of blackened fishskin bound with gilt wire. Where the knuckle-bow turned to the quillon was a shell guard, upswept and decorated with a superimposed silver grenade. The blade was of flattened diamond section about 27 in. in length. It was carried in a black leather scabbard with top and bottom mounts, the top mount being fitted with a stud for frog suspension.

H. Royal Artillery officers of the middle eighteenth century carried the regulation sword of the period, having a gilt brass hilt consisting of knuckle-bow and shells with a ball pommel. The blade being about 28 in. and straight. It was carried in a leather scabbard, black with top and bottom mounts, the top mount being fitted with a stud for carriage from a baldrick or frog.

I. Non-commissioned officers of Native Indian regiments, havildars by name, carried a sword which had a slightly curved blade and a hilt consisting of a plain brass knuckle-bow with a ball pommel and a grip bound with leather. The scabbard was invariably of leather with mounts that protected the bottom against dragging on the ground and at the top provided a guide for the blade and also a means of suspension with the fitment of a stud was held in the frog from the belt or baldrick.

SELECT BIBLIOGRAPHY

Blackmore, H. L. *British Military Firearms.* H. Jenkins, 1961

Carman, W. Y. *British Military Uniforms.* Longacre Press, 1962

    Indian Army Uniforms, Vol. 2 Infantry. Morgan Grampian, 1969

Lawson, C. C. P. *History of Uniforms of the British Army.* Kaye & Ward, 1967

Luard, J. *History of the Dress of the British Soldier.* William Clowes, 1852

Milne, S. M. *Standards and Colours of the Army.* Privately printed, 1893

Parkyn, H. G. *Shoulder Belts, Plates and Buttons.* Gale & Polden, 1956

Wilkinson-Latham, R. *British Military Bayonets 1700–1945.* Hutchinson, 1967

    British Military Swords 1800 to the Present Day. Hutchinson, 1966

See also various Regimental Histories and Dress Regulations, and Cannons Records.

INDEX